The Kids Book of
BLACK
HISTORY
in Canada

Written by Rosemary Sadlier
Illustrated by Arden Taylor

KIDS CAN PRESS

To all African and Black Canadian ancestors for their dreams, for guiding my journey and to my parents, Henry and Bernice Sadlier, for connecting me to advocacy for Black History. To my three children, Jenne, Raia and Alexander, for being a source of inspiration and support. — R.S.

In dedication to my Auntie Diana. Thank you for always supporting my artistic endeavours. Though you are no longer with us, I will always remember your strong personality and the laughter we shared. — A.T.

Acknowledgments

I am greatly indebted to Genie MacLeod, Barb Kelly, Shannon Swift, Debbie Innes and Catherine Dorton for their expertise in editing and guiding this process, as well as to Arden Taylor, who provided the amazing artwork.

African Acknowledgment by Rosemary Sadlier OOnt

I would like to acknowledge that this land was settled and supported very early by people of African descent, the first named African being translator Mathieu Da Costa by 1604, and to acknowledge the ongoing and seminal contribution made by him and those who preceded and followed in Canada's development. I acknowledge the many people of African descent who are not settlers, but whose ancestors were forcibly displaced as part of the Atlantic slave trade, brought against their will and made to work on these lands. We must acknowledge that African Canadians were an integral part of shaping Canadian history, and our history would not be the same without the Black experience.

PHOTO CREDITS

Page 39: original of newspaper article in collection of Glenbow Archives in Calgary (Photo/NA-3556-3b).

Text © 2024 Rosemary Sadlier
Illustrations © 2024 Arden Taylor

Update of *The Kids Book of Black Canadian History* © 2003

The term "Colored Corps" is used in this book to match the spelling and terminology used at the time.

Published in Canada and the U.S. by Kids Can Press Ltd.
25 Dockside Drive, Toronto, ON M5A 0B5

Kids Can Press is a Corus Entertainment Inc. company
www.kidscanpress.com

The artwork in this book was rendered digitally.
The text is set in Caecilia.

Edited by Genie MacLeod and Kathleen Keenan
Designed by Barb Kelly

Printed and bound in Buji, Shenzhen, China, in 8/2025 by WKT Company

CM 24 0 9 8 7 6 5 4 3 2

Library and Archives Canada Cataloguing in Publication

Title: The kids book of Black history in Canada / by Rosemary Sadlier ; illustrations by Arden Taylor.
Other titles: Kids book of Black Canadian history | Black history in Canada
Names: Sadlier, Rosemary, author. | Taylor, Arden, illustrator.
Description: Series statement: Kids book of | Previously published under title: The kids book of Black Canadian history. | Includes index.
Identifiers: Canadiana 2023046808X | ISBN 9781525307379 (hardcover)
Subjects: LCSH: Black people – Canada – History – Juvenile literature. | LCSH: Black people – Canada – Biography – Juvenile literature. | LCSH: Canada – Race relations – Juvenile literature. | CSH: Black Canadians – History – Juvenile literature. | CSH: Black Canadians – Biography Juvenile literature. | LCGFT: Biographies.
Classification: LCC FC106.B6 S22 2024 | DDC j971/.00496 – dc23

Kids Can Press gratefully acknowledges that the land on which our office is located is the traditional territory of many nations, including the Mississaugas of the Credit, the Anishnabeg, the Chippewa, the Haudenosaunee and the Wendat Peoples, and is now home to many diverse First Nations, Inuit and Métis Peoples.

We thank the Government of Ontario, through Ontario Creates and the Ontario Arts Council; the Canada Council for the Arts; and the Government of Canada for their financial support of our publishing activity.

Contents

What Is Black Canadian History?

Canada is one of the most diverse countries in the world. The people of Canada represent many different backgrounds — Indigenous Peoples, Senegalese, Chinese, Jamaican, Scottish, Syrian, Italian, Nigerian, Ukrainian, Indian and hundreds more. Canadian history includes the stories of all these people.

But for a long time, history books focused only on white people from Great Britain and France. That's probably because these countries were among the first to send settlers to Canada and keep records of their voyages. But Indigenous Peoples were already here when these Europeans arrived.

What about Black people? The first named African arrived in Canada about 400 years ago. Black Canadians — also called African Canadians — have changed Canada and made important contributions to its story. They have a fascinating history full of strong, courageous people.

Why Did Black People Come to Canada?

Black people have been in Canada since before it was called Canada. Some Black people arrived here as explorers. Some came as enslaved people, brought against their will by the people who enslaved them. Many came to escape slavery. Others were soldiers who helped Britain defend Canada against the French or Americans. Still more hoped to fulfill their dreams or find a place where they could live, raise their families and work or go to school.

Black Canadians Are Diverse

Black Canadians can trace their history to more than 300 different ethnic and cultural origins. Some of the most common origins for Black Canadians and their ancestors are:

- Jamaican
- British
- Nigerian
- Ethiopian
- Trinidadian/Tobagonian
- Haitian
- Somali
- French
- Scottish

African Roots

All Black people have African ancestors, whether their skin tone is light or dark. Some Black Canadians have parents, grandparents and more ancestors who were born in Canada, while others have come recently from Africa, Europe, South America, the United States, Bermuda, or Caribbean countries such as Barbados, Haiti, Jamaica or Trinidad and Tobago.

Who Are the Black Canadians?

The five main groups of Black Canadians are:
- People who have lived in Canada for several generations
- Immigrants from Bermuda, the Caribbean and South America
- Immigrants from Africa
- Immigrants from the United States
- Immigrants from Europe (especially England)

Most people in the first group originally came from the United States. But Black Canadians all share a common African heritage. Today, Black people's experiences of life in Canada connect them.

A Note on Terms

Black is usually capitalized to reflect and honour Black people's shared African identity and heritage, no matter what their skin tone or where they live in the world. In contrast, *white* has been used to describe many different groups of people throughout history and doesn't carry the same sense of shared identity, so it's not capitalized in this book.

Black Canadians in Canada

- Canada's Black population has doubled in the last twenty years.
- More than four in ten Black Canadians were born in Canada.
- The majority of Black Canadians live in metropolitan areas.
- The cities with the highest population of Black Canadians are:
  - Toronto
  - Montreal
  - Ottawa-Gatineau
  - Oshawa
  - Edmonton
  - Calgary
  - Halifax

Time to Tell the Story

For years, Canadians didn't see Black Canadians in history books, on television or in newspapers — their stories weren't told. Many people, Black or white, didn't know about Black people's important contributions to Canada. But Black Canadians have added to Canada's story in many ways. From military heroes and journalists to cowboys and activists, Black Canadians have a proud history, present and future.

Richard Pierpoint was a military hero who formed an all-Black regiment to fight in the War of 1812.

Mary Ann Shadd was the first female newspaper publisher in North America.

Harriet Tubman, a conductor on the Underground Railroad, saved more than 300 enslaved Black people.

Dr. Anderson Ruffin Abbott was the first Black graduate of Toronto's Medical College.

African Beginnings

Black Canadian history does not begin in Canada. It begins on the continent of Africa. Before the enslavement of Africans by Europeans, many great kingdoms flourished in Africa — places of learning, wealth and excellence. African merchants, sailors and explorers met people from many places, including European countries.

African kings and merchants established trade relationships with European nations to get metals and manufactured goods. Trade was attractive to Europeans who wanted gold, spices and raw minerals, and opportunities to expand markets for their goods. Africans also crossed the Atlantic Ocean with Europeans to find more wealth.

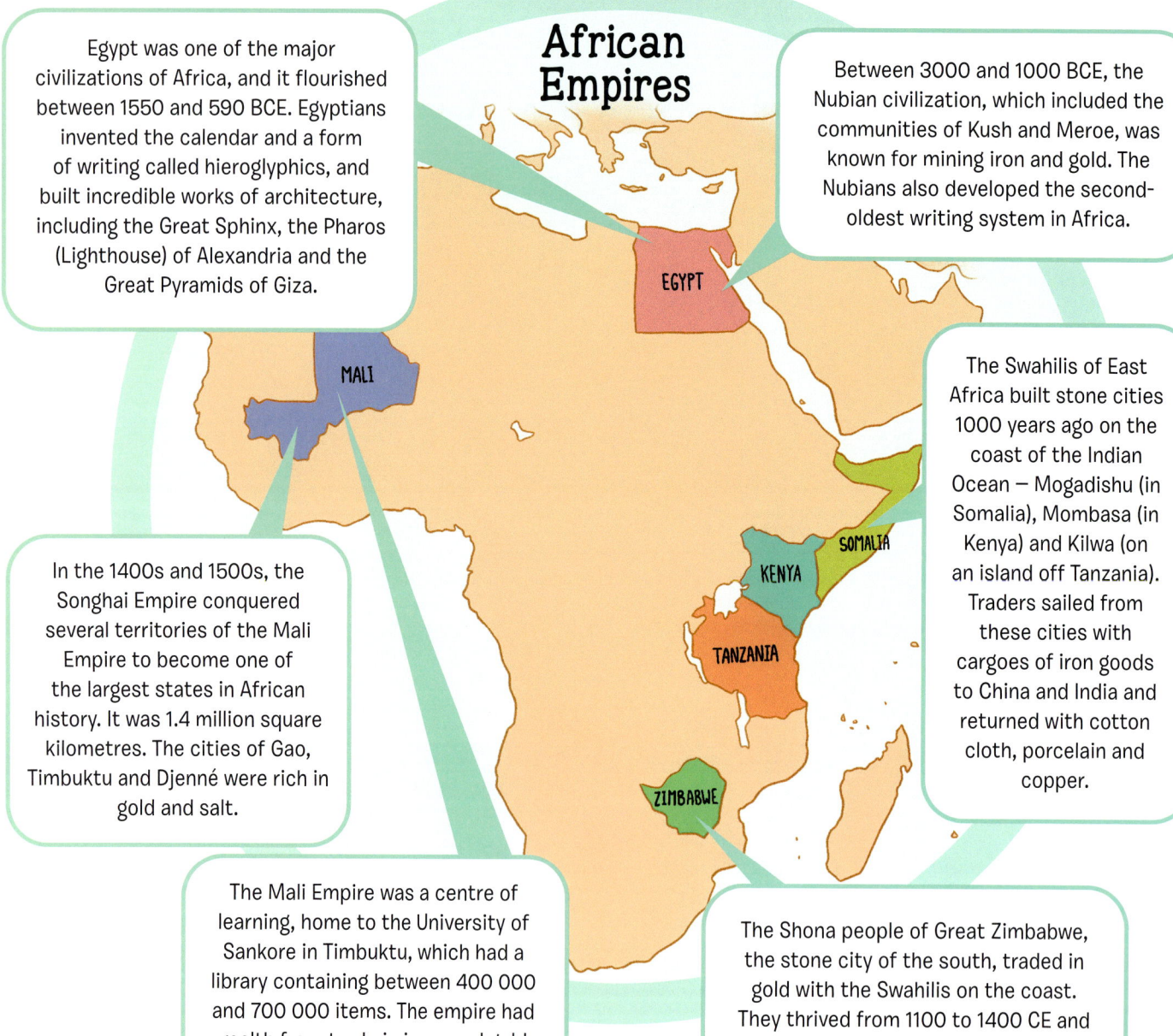

African Empires

Egypt was one of the major civilizations of Africa, and it flourished between 1550 and 590 BCE. Egyptians invented the calendar and a form of writing called hieroglyphics, and built incredible works of architecture, including the Great Sphinx, the Pharos (Lighthouse) of Alexandria and the Great Pyramids of Giza.

Between 3000 and 1000 BCE, the Nubian civilization, which included the communities of Kush and Meroe, was known for mining iron and gold. The Nubians also developed the second-oldest writing system in Africa.

In the 1400s and 1500s, the Songhai Empire conquered several territories of the Mali Empire to become one of the largest states in African history. It was 1.4 million square kilometres. The cities of Gao, Timbuktu and Djenné were rich in gold and salt.

The Swahilis of East Africa built stone cities 1000 years ago on the coast of the Indian Ocean — Mogadishu (in Somalia), Mombasa (in Kenya) and Kilwa (on an island off Tanzania). Traders sailed from these cities with cargoes of iron goods to China and India and returned with cotton cloth, porcelain and copper.

The Mali Empire was a centre of learning, home to the University of Sankore in Timbuktu, which had a library containing between 400 000 and 700 000 items. The empire had wealth from trade in ivory and gold.

The Shona people of Great Zimbabwe, the stone city of the south, traded in gold with the Swahilis on the coast. They thrived from 1100 to 1400 CE and built monuments, such as the Great Enclosure wall, from granite.

Europeans & Trade Routes

By the 1400s, Africans and Europeans came into contact frequently due to trade. Europeans valued African products like gold, palm oil, salt and pepper. Africans valued European metals, cloth, guns and cowry shells, which were a form of money. This interest in trade increased travel and contact, and the Dutch and later the Portuguese set up permanent sites in present-day Senegal and Sierra Leone and in East and South Africa.

Contact created families of mixed African and European descent who spoke Creole — languages created with words from both groups. People from these Creole communities were fluent in the languages and cultures of both groups, which made them valuable in trade and exploration.

Crossing the Atlantic

The land we now call Canada was home to Indigenous Peoples long before Europeans or Africans arrived. At first, Indigenous Peoples had little contact with the European ships that came to Canada's East Coast to fish. Later, Europeans seeking furs started to trade with local Mi'kmaq and Wolastoqiyik, exchanging wool blankets, metal tools and other manufactured goods. To make trade easier, they formed a trade language, or pidgin, blending the languages of the Mi'kmaq and Wolastoqiyik with some of the Basque, Spanish and Portuguese words of the fishermen. Some early European explorers arrived with Africans on board who learned this transatlantic trade language.

Did You Know

Africans were also explorers. In the 1300s, a wealthy Malian king, Mansa Musa, sent an exploration party to the West, across the Atlantic Ocean.

An African Trader in Canada

One African Creole who travelled with Europeans, Mathieu Da Costa, was a free West African man with many skills. Because Da Costa was hired as a navigator and dealmaker by Europeans, his name appears in French, Portuguese and Dutch records, making him the first "named" African in Canada. In about 1604, he landed on Canada's East Coast. He worked for Samuel de Champlain and Pierre Dugua de Mons, assisting with mapping and creating trade deals between the French and Indigenous Peoples. He was part of the 1606 social club "Order of Good Cheer." Da Costa could speak Mi'kmaq as well as French, English, Dutch and Portuguese, so he was in high demand among European traders.

Mathieu Da Costa, a free West African man who worked as a navigator and dealmaker

The Atlantic Slave Trade

In 1498, Vasco da Gama, an explorer from Portugal, became the first European to sail around Africa. With great excitement, he discovered some of Africa's wealthy cities. After his voyage, trade between Africa and Europe increased rapidly. Portugal, Britain and other countries wanted to trade for African gold, silk and ivory.

Soon, Portuguese and other European merchants began to buy and sell enslaved Africans as well. At that time, slavery was common around the world. Enslaved people were usually criminals or prisoners of war and could be of any race. In Africa, enslaved people were forced to work in salt mines and as porters on trade caravans. But according to law, these enslaved Africans could purchase their freedom after some years.

Plantations of the Americas

In 1492, Christopher Columbus sailed across the Atlantic Ocean from Spain and landed on a Caribbean island. He was trying to reach Asia, but had come instead to what he thought was a "New World." Of course, it wasn't a new world to the Indigenous Peoples living there.

The island's tropical climate gave the Spanish an idea: they set up huge farms, called plantations, to grow sugar cane there. These plantations needed many workers, so the Spanish owners forced the Indigenous people into slavery. But many of the enslaved people fled or died from European diseases, such as smallpox and measles.

By 1600, the Portuguese, British, French and Dutch also had plantations and mines in the Caribbean and the Americas. They all wanted workers, and so they turned to the slave traders. In Africa, both Africans and Europeans rounded up men and women and marched them in chains to coastal cities. There they were crammed into ships and sent across the Atlantic Ocean. The Atlantic slave trade became a huge business for the enslavers who profited.

Transatlantic Trade Route

- Enslaved Black people are shipped from Africa to colonies in the Caribbean and the Americas.

- Raw materials, such as sugar and gold, are sent from the colonies back to Europe.

- Manufactured goods, such as guns and cotton cloth, are sent to Africa in trade for the enslaved people.

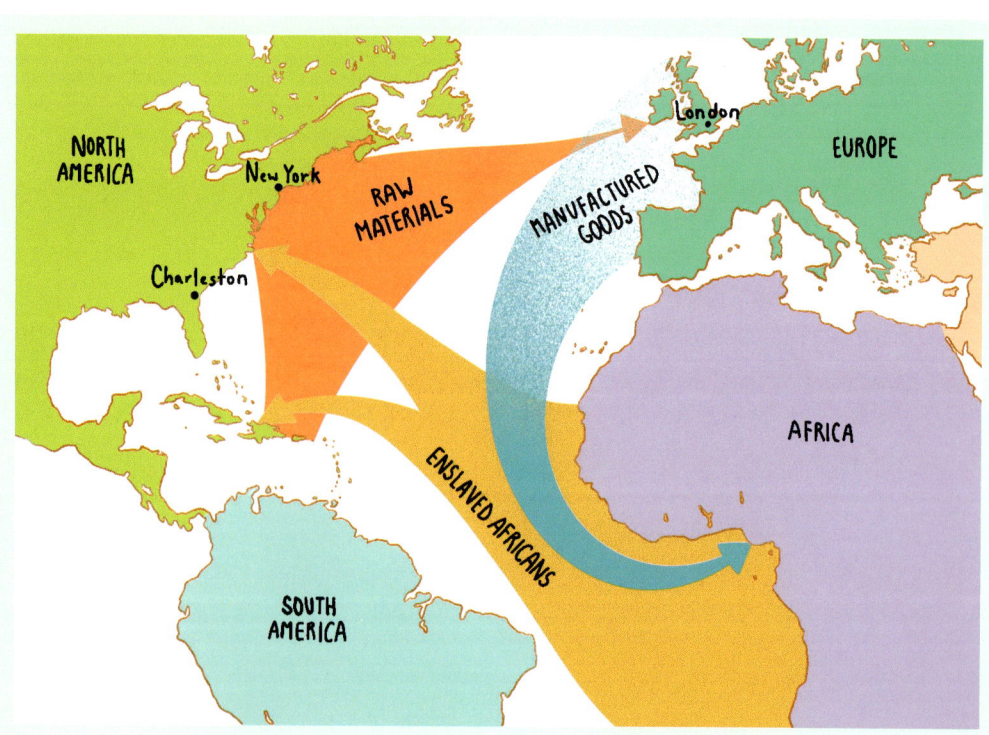

The Slave Ships

Conditions on the slave ships were hideous. Before boarding, the captives were branded like cattle so that their purchasers could identify them on arrival. Once on board, they were packed in so closely they could barely move. Afraid of revolts, sailors guarded the captives with guns. There were terrible shortages of drinking water and food during the voyages. Many enslaved people became sick and died.

"[The captives] were all enclosed under grated hatchways between decks. The space was so low that they sat between each other's legs, and stowed so close together that there was no possibility of lying down, or at all changing their positions, by night or by day."

– report from a British anti-slaving patrol in 1829

Effects of the Slave Trade

The Atlantic slave trade lasted 250 years, from about 1600 to 1850. At least 20 million Black people were taken from Africa to the Americas, the Caribbean, China, Europe and other countries. Historians say that 10 to 12 million captives landed alive in the Americas and Caribbean. Almost one-third of all Black people died during the passage.

The effect on Africa was devastating, as communities lost generations of their young people. The colonies gained from the skills the Africans brought with them, including their knowledge of tropical agriculture, healing and carpentry. Others contributed music and other arts to the culture of their new home.

PROFILE : Abu Bakr al-Siddiq

Most enslaved Africans who crossed the Atlantic Ocean never saw their homes again. Abu Bakr al-Siddiq was an exception. Born in Timbuktu in 1790, he was brought up in a well-educated Muslim family, then captured and sent to Jamaica as a slave. There, his owner discovered that he could read and write Arabic (like many other enslaved people). As a result, al-Siddiq was freed after 30 years of slavery. He joined an English expedition to Timbuktu and managed to return home.

Issue: Slavery

A slave is a human being who is considered to be the property of another person. Enslaved people are forced to work and to live in poor conditions and are not free to make decisions about their own lives. In the slave trade, people were bought and sold like cattle at a farm market.

In the past, slavery was common in many countries. For instance, white Europeans enslaved other white Europeans, and some Indigenous nations had slaves. If you were taken prisoner in a battle, or if you owed someone a lot of money, you might be made a slave. Usually, slaves could work hard and purchase their freedom. Slavery didn't necessarily last for a lifetime.

When Africans were captured and shipped to the Americas, however, things changed. The Africans were enslaved for their entire lives, and their children were the owner's property. There was no way they could buy their freedom. For these Black people, slavery was a permanent condition.

African Culture in the Americas

In the Caribbean and South America, enslaved Black people far outnumbered white people. As a result, they were able to keep alive their African songs, languages and religions. In the United States, however, much of African culture was soon forgotten by the children and grandchildren of the enslaved Black people. Canada had a small population of enslaved people, and their heritage also was mostly forgotten.

American Plantations

A plantation is a large farm that grows one crop, such as cotton, sugar or coffee. Most plantations are in tropical countries or places with hot climates, such as the southern United States. Plantation owners needed many workers. Most owned 10 to 20 enslaved Black people, but some of the richer ones had 100 or more. Because enslaved people were forced to work for free, the owners could make large profits.

The enslaved Africans who lived on American plantations had no rights. They weren't allowed to go to school or learn to read and write, nor could they legally marry or go anywhere without their owner's permission. As well, enslaved people were punished or sold whenever their owner liked.

Working in the Fields

Most male and many female enslaved people toiled in the fields. They worked 16-hour days, from sunrise to sundown, six days a week. Supervised by overseers — white men or other enslaved people trusted by the owner — they hoed, planted or harvested crops under the hot sun. The overseers took any opportunity to punish enslaved people. If an enslaved person arrived late, made a mistake or worked too slowly, they could receive 50 to 100 lashes from the overseer's whip.

Other Slave Work

About one-quarter of enslaved Black people were domestic workers or tradespeople such as carpenters, builders and weavers. The domestic workers, or "house slaves," worked in the owner's house, performing tasks for the owner's wife and family. Most were children, women or old people, and they worked as cooks, caregivers, grooms and drivers. They had to do whatever their owner demanded. If they angered the owner, they could be whipped.

Family Life

Enslaved families lived in small cabins away from the owner's house. They often had six or seven children, who had to begin working when they were just seven- or eight-years-old.

Some enslaved families had garden plots and could grow their own food. They also hunted and fished to get enough to eat. Singing, dancing, storytelling and practising their religion helped keep their culture alive. Sundays were free, and Christmas brought a few days' holiday.

PROFILE : Josiah Henson

Josiah Henson was born enslaved in Maryland in 1789. When he was about three, his father tried to protect his mother from a vicious beating. For this crime, his father had an ear cut off, was whipped and was sold to a new owner.

Henson and his mother were purchased by a Kentucky farmer called Isaac Riley. When Henson grew up, he was made manager of Riley's farm.

While still enslaved, Henson became a Christian preacher. But the cruelty of slavery was becoming unbearable. When he was 20, an overseer broke both his shoulder blades in a beating. Two years later, Henson married a young enslaved woman named Charlotte and started a family. He began to think about escaping.

Henson finally made his break for freedom in 1830 after Riley broke his promise to free him. He and Charlotte and their children set out on a long, terrifying journey from Kentucky. (Read more about Henson on pages 25, 28 and 30).

The Auction Block

In their lifetime, most enslaved people would live on two or more plantations. When an owner decided to sell an enslaved person, he took them to a market, where they were closely examined by purchasers. Some owners employed a slave trader to help them with these sales. The trader would feed the enslaved people just enough so that they looked healthy at sale time.

It was common for enslaved families to be split up when sold. Children were separated from parents, and husbands from wives. Often, they never saw one another again. Enslaved people who were moving to a new plantation marched in "coffles" — lines of people chained together. Many died before they arrived.

Slave auctions were frequent in Canada as well, especially in Nova Scotia. In the 1700s, newspapers regularly advertised sales of skilled enslaved people.

"When I was 15-years-old, I was brought to the courthouse, put up on the auction block to be sold. Old Judge Miller was there. I knew him well because he was one of the wealthiest slave owners in the county and the meanest one … I spoke right out on the auction block and told him: 'Judge Miller! Don't you bid for me, 'cause if you do, I would not live on your plantation. I will take a knife and cut my own throat from ear to ear before I would be owned by you.'"

– Delicia Patterson, an enslaved Black American girl

Religion on the Plantations

For the first 100 years of slavery, white owners didn't want enslaved workers to become Christians. But by the mid-1700s, many Black people began to join Protestant churches, especially Baptist and Methodist. Soon, Black people were turning church services into joyous occasions full of music and movement.

Some plantation owners tried to control enslaved people through religion. They would bring a white Christian minister to preach to the enslaved people. The message? That obedience to the owner was a good thing, and enslaved people should be happy to be enslaved.

But the enslaved people understood Christianity in a different way. In the Bible, they read about the enslaved Jews in Egypt. They believed that God had sent Moses to free the Jews from their owners, and they longed for the same freedom.

Spirituals

In their religious songs, called spirituals, enslaved people sang about their hopes of becoming free or going to heaven. Later, when enslaved people were escaping to Canada, these songs contained coded messages to help them travel the Underground Railroad.

Let My People Go

When Israel was in Egypt's land,
Let my people go,
Oppressed so hard they could not stand,
Let my people go.

Go down, Moses,
Way down in Egypt land,
Tell ole Pharaoh,
Let my people go.

Life for Enslaved People in Canada

Most enslaved Black people in early Canada were domestic workers. Besides cleaning the owner's house, doing the laundry and preparing meals, they cared for children and old people, made clothing, candles and soap, and tended small vegetable gardens. Some developed trades such as carpentry, blacksmithing and hairdressing. Others helped to clear the land, chop logs and store firewood in preparation for the long, cold winters.

The Fight Against Slavery

There were always people who objected to slavery. They were called abolitionists because they wanted to end, or abolish, slavery. One group was the Quakers in the northern American colonies. Quakers were Christians who felt that all people deserved liberty in the eyes of God.

In Britain, too, there were strong opponents to slavery, such as William Wilberforce, a Member of Parliament (MP). In Upper Canada (now Ontario), Lieutenant-Governor John Graves Simcoe took a big step toward abolishing slavery in 1793. (Read more about Simcoe on page 17.)

After Slavery

When the Civil War broke out in the United States in 1861, many enslaved people in the South escaped to fight for the North. Two years later, President Abraham Lincoln signed the Emancipation Proclamation, making slavery illegal in the U.S. After the North won the war in 1865, all enslaved people in America were declared free, although many slave owners tried to hide the news from enslaved people.

Did You Know

In 1831, Nat Turner, an enslaved man from Virginia, led a rebellion during which more than 60 white people were killed. Soldiers were called in to stop the rebellion. The incident led to harsher laws in the American South that restricted the movement of enslaved people. As a result, many enslaved people tried to escape to Canada – by that time, slavery was illegal here.

Did You Know

Slavery still exists today in a number of countries. Many enslaved people today are children who have been kidnapped or purchased from impoverished parents. They are forced to work in factories and mines, on farms or construction sites, in people's homes or as child soldiers.

Slavery in New France

While the Atlantic slave trade was growing, Europeans were exploring the northern parts of North America. John Cabot, who was born in Italy (where he was known as Giovanni Caboto), sailed to Canada's east coast from Bristol, England, in 1497.

Britain claimed ownership of North America after Cabot's voyage, even though Indigenous Peoples had been living on the land for thousands of years. Another 100 years passed before Britain founded its first colony, Virginia, in what's now the United States. Then, in 1608, the explorer Samuel de Champlain established a colony for France at what is now Quebec City. Over the next 150 years, this colony — New France — grew, and its population reached about 65 000.

NEW FRANCE

⬤ New France

Who Was Enslaved?

The first enslaved people in New France were people of the Pawnee Nation, called panis by the French. But many of the enslaved Indigenous people were killed by European diseases. So the French settlers imported enslaved Africans from American and Caribbean plantations. The Africans had built up immunity to most European diseases. Plus, slave owners felt that the darker skin of Africans wouldn't blend in with those around them if they escaped.

There weren't many enslaved Africans in New France, however. The long, cold winters prevented the settlers from creating large plantations like the ones in the South. Their small farms didn't need many workers.

The First Enslaved African

The first enslaved African in New France was a young boy from Madagascar, off Africa's east coast. At age seven, he was sold into slavery to the British commander David Kirke. When Kirke invaded Quebec City in 1628, he sold the boy to the colony's head clerk, Olivier LeTardif.

New France was handed back to the French in 1632. LeTardif had to flee because he had worked for the British, but he sold the enslaved boy first. The boy was educated in a school run by a Jesuit priest, Father Le Jeune. Later, the boy was baptized Olivier Le Jeune — his first name came from Olivier LeTardif and his last name from Father Le Jeune. Olivier Le Jeune died when he was 30.

Slave Labour

The labour conditions for enslaved people in New France were less harsh than on the plantations in the South. Most enslaved people lived in the cities of Montreal and Quebec and worked in people's houses. They washed and ironed clothes, cooked meals and cared for children. Some of the men worked as farm labourers.

Things were different outside the cities, however, where heavy outdoor work was needed. For example, enslaved Black people helped to build and protect French fur-trading posts.

All sorts of people were slave owners — military men, merchants, governors and priests. Even Catholic women's convents used enslaved people in their hospitals and schools.

Enslaved people were at the lowest level of society. Their owners could beat them whenever they wished. Many died young, at an average age of 25. By 1760, New France's population of 65 000 included about 1200 enslaved Black people and 2500 panis.

Did You Know

Although slavery wasn't legal in France, the Code Noir (Black Code) made it acceptable in New France. Passed by King Louis XIV of France, the Black Code stated how enslaved people were to be treated. Slavery was made fully legal in New France in 1709.

Marie-Joseph Angélique

Marie-Joseph Angélique's story shows how harshly enslaved people could be punished. Angélique was enslaved as a domestic worker in Montreal. In April 1734, she learned that she was about to be sold and decided to run away. While she was escaping, a fire started in her owner's house. The flames spread and destroyed 46 homes. Angélique was arrested and found guilty of starting the fire. She was tortured, paraded through the streets and hanged.

PROFILE : Marie Marguerite Rose

Marie Marguerite Rose was one of the first enslaved Africans in Canada during the French Regime. At 19, she was captured in Africa and forced into slavery at Ile Royale, today's Nova Scotia. Freed 19 years later at age 38, she married Jean Pierre Laurent, a Mi'kmaw man, and together they ran a thriving tavern in Louisbourg until her death in 1757. She is an early example of enslaved Black women's resilience, and her story shows how her skills as a businessperson helped her.

Slavery in British Canada

In 1763, France lost its Seven Years' War with Britain, and New France became a British colony called Quebec. For enslaved Black and Indigenous people, little changed under British rule. Enslaved people were still considered the property of their owners and had no rights of their own.

General James Murray, the first British governor of Quebec, was a slave owner. So were several other government officials. Many more enslaved Black people would arrive in British Canada, and several decades would pass before slavery ended.

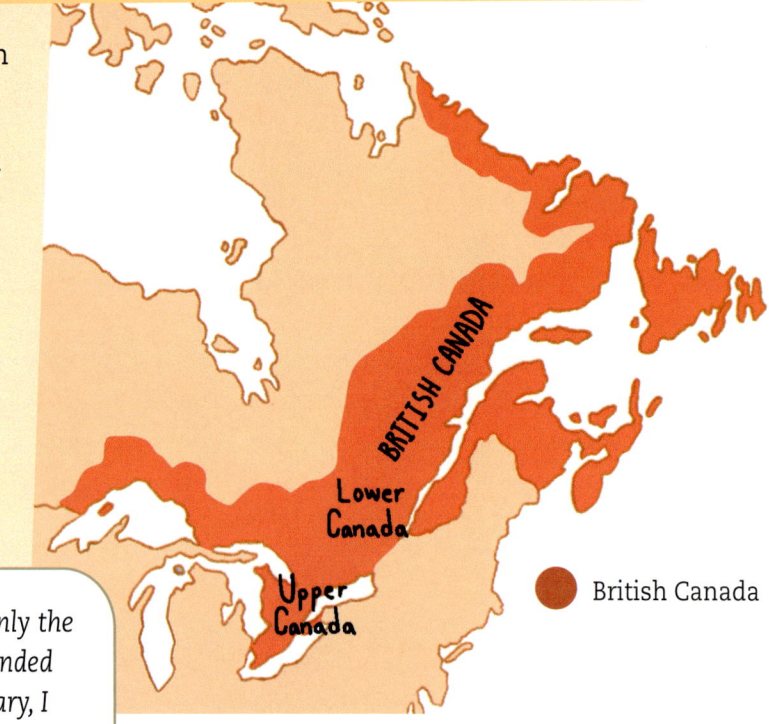

British Canada

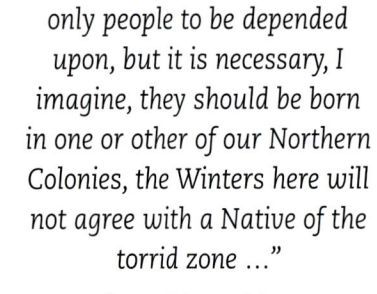

"Black Slaves are certainly the only people to be depended upon, but it is necessary, I imagine, they should be born in one or other of our Northern Colonies, the Winters here will not agree with a Native of the torrid zone ..."

– General James Murray

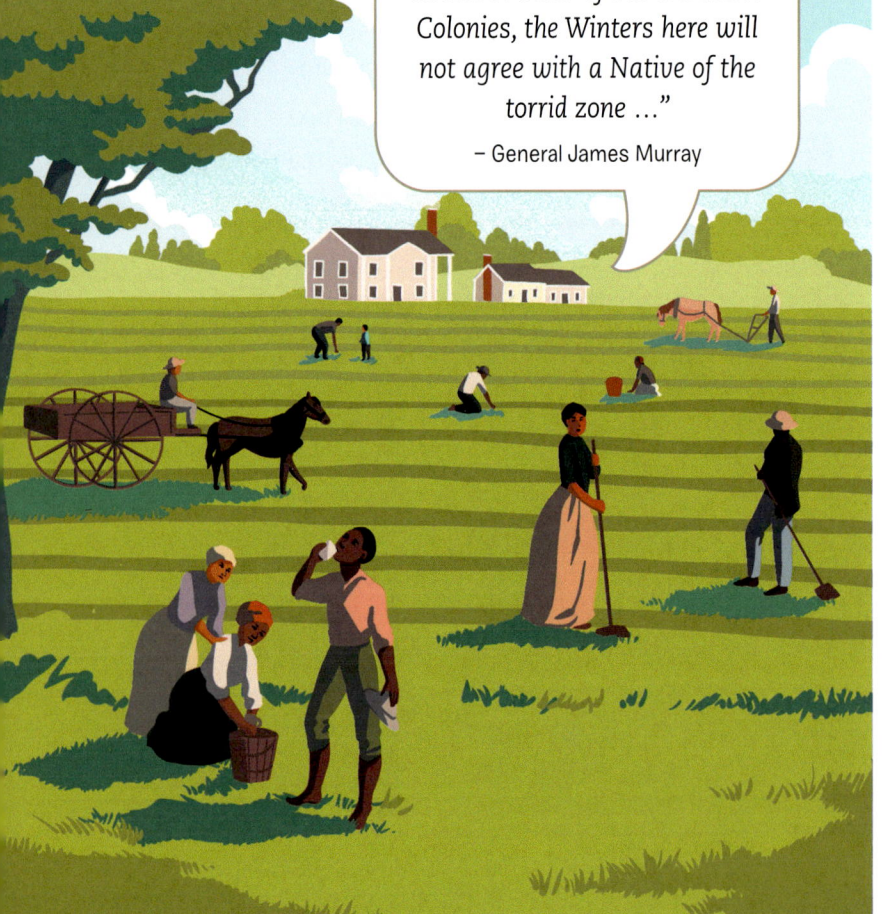

Nova Scotia and Prince Edward Island

Nova Scotia became a British colony in 1749. Settlers arriving from New England brought enslaved people with them, and enslaved Black people helped to build the city of Halifax. By 1767, there were more than 100 enslaved people in Nova Scotia. Newspapers such as the *Nova Scotia Advertiser* and the *Royal Gazette* advertised slave auctions and published notices offering rewards for enslaved people who escaped.

A much smaller number of enslaved people lived in the colony of Isle St. Jean (which became Prince Edward Island in 1799). Two enslaved Black people came with a merchant from New York. A few more were owned by Colonel Joseph Robinson from North Carolina. Slavery continued in Prince Edward Island until 1825.

Upper Canada

In 1791, Britain divided the enormous Province of Quebec into Lower Canada (now Quebec) and Upper Canada (now Ontario). At that time, there were still enslaved Black people living in both colonies. The man who governed Upper Canada from 1796, Peter Russell, was a slave owner.

Another slave owner in Upper Canada was Joseph Brant. He was a famous Kanyen'kehà:ka (Mohawk) chief who was loyal to Britain during the American Revolution (also called the War of American Independence). As a reward, Brant received a large grant of land in what's now southwestern Ontario. He owned about 30 enslaved people, but he also allowed free Black people to live on his land and marry people in his tribe.

Justifying Slavery

It's hard to understand how one group of people could enslave another. When the African slave trade began, many European people felt guilty about the way they were treating their captives. They and some white settlers in the colonies tried to justify the slave trade. Many felt that it was permissible because it made them money. Others argued that the Africans were uncivilized savages and — even worse — pagans (not Christians).

But most enslaved Black people became Christians in the Americas. Then white Christians who supported slavery looked in the Bible for new arguments. Some claimed that Black people were the descendants of Ham, a man condemned to be a servant.

Such false theories of Black inferiority are racist and, unfortunately, persist today.

PROFILE : John Graves Simcoe

John Graves Simcoe was the lieutenant-governor, or leader, of Upper Canada from 1792 to 1796. Born in England, Simcoe was good at sports and popular in school. After joining the army, he was sent overseas to fight as a British commander during the American Revolution. Later, in the British Parliament, Simcoe spoke out against slavery.

When Simcoe settled in Newark (now Niagara-on-the-Lake), in Upper Canada, he was shocked to hear about the case of Chloë Cooley, an enslaved Black girl from nearby Queenston. Cooley had been tied up by her owner, thrown into a boat and taken across the Niagara River to the United States to be sold.

Simcoe's government quickly passed a law, in 1793, to limit slavery. The law said that any child born to an enslaved person in Upper Canada would become free at age 25, and that no new enslaved people could be brought into the province. After this, slavery slowly began to disappear in Upper Canada.

Black Loyalists in the Maritimes

In 1775, a war broke out in America that brought many people — Black and white — to Britain's east-coast Canadian colonies, the Maritimes.

The Thirteen Colonies in America, discontented with British rule, were battling for their independence. After a long and bitter struggle, the Americans won the American Revolution in 1783. This led to the founding of the United States of America. But while many Americans were celebrating the birth of the United States, thousands of others were leaving for a new life in Canada.

Did You Know

Birchtown was named after General Samuel Birch. Birch was the British officer who protected the Black Loyalists in New York after the American Revolution and signed most of their Certificates of Freedom.

Canada — A Safe Haven

During the American Revolution, Canada became known as a safe place for Black people. Slavery still existed, but the British promised freedom and land in Canada to all Black people who fought on their side in the war. They did this because they needed allies. Also, the British wanted to ensure that the Canadian colonies wouldn't join the Americans in their fight for independence.

Attracted by the British offer, thousands of enslaved people ran away from their plantations and joined up.

Black Loyalists

Americans who stayed loyal to Britain during the Revolution were called United Empire Loyalists. After Britain's defeat, 30 000 Loyalists gathered in New York and set sail for Nova Scotia. About 3500 were Black people who had been given their freedom. Another 1500 were enslaved Black people brought by white Loyalists.

Looking forward to a new life, most of the free Black Loyalists settled in Nova Scotia and New Brunswick. Others travelled to Upper and Lower Canada (now Ontario and Quebec).

Birchtown

In 1784, Birchtown, Nova Scotia, was the largest free Black town outside of Africa, with a population of more than 1500 people.

Despite being overcrowded, Birchtown developed a strong community life. Like other Maritime Black people, Birchtown residents often gathered to work, visit or attend church services.

Other Black Communities

Black settlements were built outside other towns in the Maritimes because that's where Black people were given land. Preston and Digby, in Nova Scotia, had Black settlements, and Charlottetown, in Prince Edward Island, had the Bog. Near Saint John, New Brunswick, Black people established small centres such as Loch Lomond, Willow Grove and Elm Hill.

Churches

Churches — Baptist, Methodist and Anglican — were a big part of life for Black Loyalists in Nova Scotia. British and Canadian charitable groups helped build and support Black churches. David George, a Black activist and reformer, built Baptist churches all over Nova Scotia using money the Black community donated.

Waiting for Land

Many Black Loyalists waited up to five years for the land they'd been promised. If they did receive it, their plots were half the size offered to the white people. The soil was thin and rocky, and farming was very difficult.

In Birchtown, community leaders Thomas Peters and Murphy Still protested the long waits. Both men were former Black Pioneers. Perhaps for that reason, they succeeded in getting land for themselves. But many Black settlers never received the farms that had been promised to them.

Disappointment

Black Loyalists who had no land were forced to work for white farmers or merchants to earn money. They were poor, mistreated and even denied the right to vote. Birchtown and other Black communities began to look like refugee camps rather than successful towns.

Schools and Self-Help

British charities assisted with the building of schools in Black communities. Colonel Blucke became a teacher at one of these schools in Birchtown. He hoped that education would enable his people to prosper. Inspired by activists such as David George, Black people formed self-help organizations and anti-slavery groups. Much later, in the 1960s, these groups would join the civil rights movement, which began in the United States, to demand equal rights for all Black people.

PROFILE : The Black Pioneers

The only all-Black British regiment in the American Revolution was the Black Pioneers. In the army, a pioneer was a soldier who did tasks including clearing ground for camps, removing obstructions and digging trenches. Black men weren't permitted to serve as regular soldiers.

After the war, the Black Pioneers settled in Nova Scotia. They helped to design and build the town of Shelburne. Many white Loyalists moved there, but the land grants the Pioneers and their leader, Colonel Stephen Blucke, received were located outside of Shelburne. There, they built Birchtown, where other Black Loyalists soon joined them.

Back to Africa

Many Black Loyalists were unhappy in the Maritimes. They were frustrated by the lack of decent land and work. When a message of hope came, they were ready for it. That message came in 1791 from Thomas Peters, a former Black Pioneer. Peters had sailed from Nova Scotia to England to complain to the British government about the Black Loyalists' situation.

While in London, Peters met members of an anti-slavery organization. They were looking for Black settlers to form a new colony in Africa. When Peters returned to Birchtown, he and an Englishman, Lieutenant John Clarkson, convinced many people that this would be a good opportunity. So, in January 1792, 1200 of the original Black Loyalists — more than one-third — sailed for Sierra Leone. Most had never seen Africa before.

Sierra Leone

Sierra Leone is a small West African country. Granville Sharp, a British abolitionist, established a colony there in 1787 for 2000 former enslaved people from Britain and America. Others joined them, including some Africans rescued from slave ships and the Nova Scotian Black Loyalists. Conditions were difficult — food was scarce and local people were unfriendly — but the Black Canadians never returned to Canada. (Sierra Leone remained under British control until 1961, then became an independent country.)

The Jamaican Maroons

The Maritimes were about to receive other Black immigrants. In Jamaica, a group of fearless Black fighters had been defending their freedom from the British for years. The Maroons were enslaved Africans who had escaped from the Spanish in the 1600s. From their mountain hideouts, they fought off attackers for 100 years.

The British conquered Jamaica in the early 1700s, but they couldn't conquer the Maroons. Like guerrilla fighters, the Maroons launched surprise raids, then disappeared into the mountains. But in 1795, with the help of vicious attack dogs, the British tricked them into surrendering. One year later, the British government forced 600 Maroons onto ships destined for the colony of Nova Scotia.

Did You Know

"Maroon," a name for an escaped enslaved person, may come from the Spanish-American word *cimarron*, which means "living on the mountaintops."

The Maroons in Nova Scotia

When the Maroons arrived in Halifax in 1796, stories of their bravery circulated around the town. Nova Scotia's Governor Wentworth welcomed them, saying they added cheerfulness and energy to the colony. He made sure the newcomers had places to live and gave them work constructing a fortress called the Citadel. At first, both jobs and housing were paid for by the Jamaican government.

Over the next four years, things went wrong. The local people disliked the Maroons' independent spirit and disapproved of their "un-Christian" ways. Since the Maroons were given jobs, homes and provisions, the locals also felt the Maroons got better treatment than they did. The Maroons, in turn, disliked the cold climate and poor food. They got frostbite the first winter and couldn't grow their favourite crops of yams, bananas, cocoa and peppers.

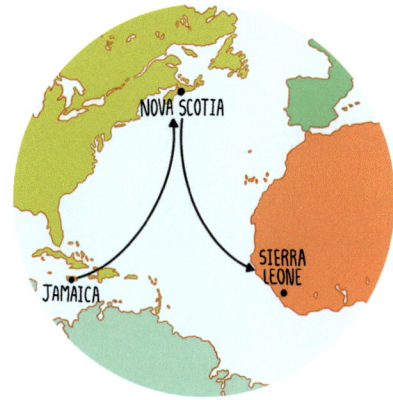

Travels from Jamaica to Nova Scotia, Canada, and then back to Sierra Leone, Africa

On to Sierra Leone

Finally, the Maroon colonel, Montague James, petitioned the government to save his people from their "miserable situation" and send them to a warmer climate. To back up the demand, the Maroons refused to work.

The British and Nova Scotian governments considered their options. The money from Jamaica was running out, and conflicts were still simmering between the Maroons and other Halifax residents. It was decided that the Maroons would go to Sierra Leone, and in August 1800, 550 of them set sail for Africa. They never returned to Canada.

Belongings of a Maroon

The British government gave these provisions to one Maroon family, Major and Mrs. John Jarrett and their daughter, when they arrived in Halifax:

24 handkerchiefs
2 coats
21 blankets
4 vests
3 walking sticks
1 box of trinkets
1 pair of trousers
16 gowns
6 shirts

15 petticoats
4 pairs of stockings
3 pairs of shoes
2 men's hats
2 women's hats
2 towels
1 tablecloth
bedding
miscellaneous

PROFILE : Nanny of the Maroons

Nanny is a national hero in Jamaica. A fearless warrior, she led the Maroons in their fight against the British in the early 1700s. Nanny was a small, wiry woman with piercing eyes. The legends say that she was especially skilled in planning sneak attacks to catch her enemies off guard.

Nanny was also a wise woman of her village. She encouraged her people to preserve the customs, music and songs they had brought from Africa. Even after Nanny died in 1734, her love of freedom encouraged Black Jamaicans to continue their struggle toward independence.

The Colored Corps

At the start of the 1800s, many enslaved people in America longed to escape to Upper Canada. In 1793, the province's lieutenant-governor, John Graves Simcoe, had promised that any enslaved Black people who entered the province would be granted their freedom.

On plantations in the American South, worried owners tried to frighten enslaved people with tales about the terrible things that would happen to them if they went to Canada. But a trickle of Black Americans began to make the difficult journey north. Upper Canada's small Black population, which still included about 1000 enslaved people, grew as the new arrivals put down roots.

Preparing for War

In the early 1800s, Black people in Upper Canada began to hear rumours of a new war between Britain and the United States. They feared that, if the Americans won, slavery would return to their province. So Richard Pierpoint, a Black Loyalist, made a plan to help defeat the Americans. In 1812, he wrote to the government asking to form an all-Black military unit to fight for Britain.

Permission was granted. The unit Pierpoint formed was put under the command of a white officer, Captain Robert Runchey, and was called Captain Runchey's Company of Colored Men, or the Colored Corps. The Black officers were Sergeants James Watters and Edward Gough, with Corporals Humphrey Waters, Francis Willson and William Thomas.

Britain and the United States at War Again

In 1812, 30 years after winning the American Revolution, the Americans declared war on Britain again. One of the main reasons was that the British, who were fighting France for control of the oceans, had stopped and searched American ships. The Americans began by attacking the closest British colonies — Upper and Lower Canada.

President Thomas Jefferson said that conquering Canada would be "a mere question of marching." He was wrong. Canadian soldiers — both Black and white — defended their country fiercely.

Valour in Battle

The Colored Corps was a valued part of the British and Canadian forces and successfully fought the Americans in a number of battles. In Upper Canada, these included Fort George, Niagara Town, Stoney Creek and Lundy's Lane. The Corps also played an important role at Queenston Heights, the most famous battle of the war.

Many other Black volunteers fought with white military units. Thousands of formerly enslaved Americans — promised freedom and land by the British — arrived to fight as well.

Who Won the War of 1812?

During the War of 1812, British and Canadian troops, joined by Black Americans and soldiers from Indigenous nations, captured several American forts, including Detroit, and burned the White House to the ground. However, neither side won, and the war ended in a stalemate in 1814. But by fighting together to keep the Americans out, Canadians of all backgrounds began to feel a new sense of pride.

Near Niagara Falls, in Queenston Park, a national historic monument commemorates the achievements of the Colored Corps.

Fort George • Queenston Heights • Lundy's Lane • Stoney Creek • NIAGARA FALLS

Black Veterans

After the War of 1812, the new lieutenant-governor of Upper Canada, Sir Peregrine Maitland, rewarded about 70 veterans of the Colored Corps with land in Oro township, near Barrie, Ontario. Maitland opposed slavery — he refused to return escaped enslaved people to their owners in the American South, and he stopped American slave catchers at the border.

Nova Scotia and New Brunswick offered Black war veterans freedom and protection, so about 2000 of them settled there. Many Black Maritimers are descendants of those American veterans.

PROFILE : Richard Pierpoint

Richard Pierpoint was a true Black Canadian hero. He was born in 1744 in Bondou, Senegal, Africa. At 16, he was captured by slave traders and sent to America. During the American Revolution, Pierpoint fought on the British side.

In 1780, Pierpoint settled near Niagara Falls and became one of Upper Canada's first pioneers. His Colored Corps was Canada's first all-Black military unit, starting a tradition that continued until World War II. When Pierpoint was an old man, he asked the government for money so that he could go home to Africa. Instead, he received a 40 ha (100 acre) farm along the Grand River (near Guelph, Ontario). He lived there, with a few other African families, until his death at the age of 94 in 1838.

The Underground Railroad

The story of the Underground Railroad is filled with daring escapes, secret passwords, disguises and brave heroes. The name makes it sound as if it was a modern subway, but it wasn't a railroad at all, and "Underground" meant "secret." It was a network of trails that enslaved people could follow from the plantations in the American South to freedom in Canada.

Along these trails, the Underground Railroad offered "stations," or safe houses, where the freedom-seekers could hide from slave catchers. Most important, the Railroad was staffed by "conductors" — women and men, Black and white. These guides defied the law to help enslaved people from southern states escape to the 14 free northern states or to Canada.

When Did It Operate?

The Underground Railroad dates from about 1831, the year of Nat Turner's revolt against slavery, to 1865, when slavery was abolished in the United States. During that time, slavery was illegal in the northern states, but Black people escaping from southern states often didn't dare to stop there. If they did, they could be caught by slave catchers, who were allowed to recapture escaped enslaved people and send them back to their owners.

Even worse, in 1850 the Fugitive Slave Act was passed. It declared that anyone in a free northern state who knew of escaped enslaved people, or "fugitives," had to turn them in. As a result, the Underground Railroad was most active in the 1850s.

Code Words

The people helping "passengers" had to communicate by mail, and letters could always be opened by others. So these code words weren't just for fun – they helped confuse slave catchers.

Promised land or Canaan	Canada (in the Bible, Canaan was the promised land to which Moses led the Jews out of slavery in Egypt)
Station	safe house on the route north
Freight or cargo	freedom-seeking enslaved people
Station masters or agents	people who helped hide freedom-seekers and directed them to the next station
Conductors	people who acted as guides and travelled with the freedom-seekers
Stockholders	people who donated money, food or transportation to freedom-seekers

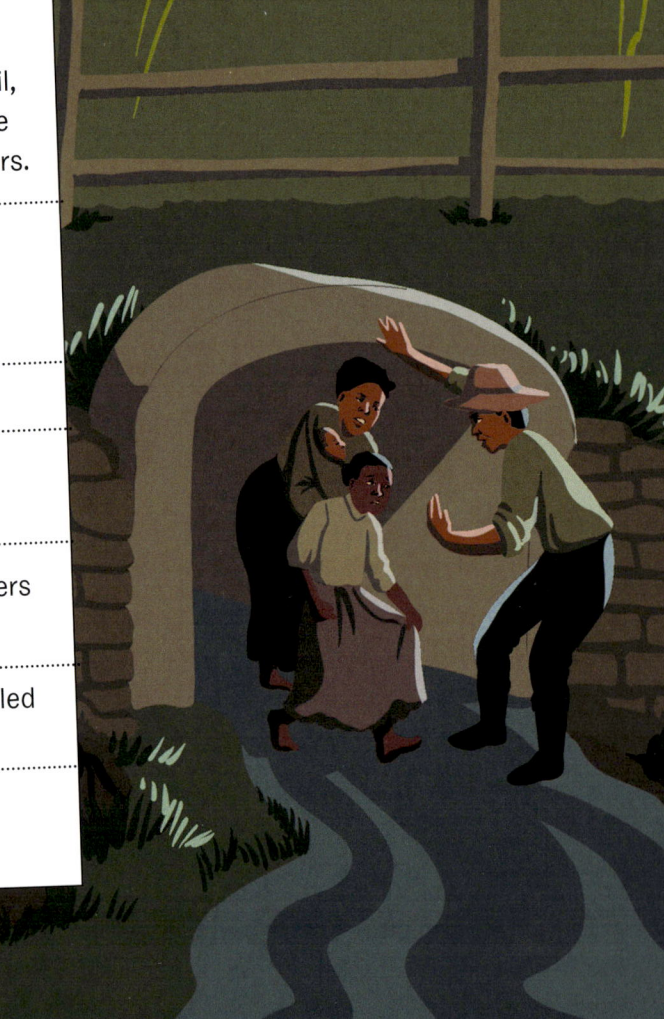

Josiah Henson's Escape

When Josiah Henson and his family escaped in 1830 from the Kentucky plantation where they lived, they took only a small parcel of food and 25 cents. Henson carried the youngest children in a sack on his back. By day, the family hid from the slave catchers. By night, they picked their way through thick woods and swamps. Guided by the North Star, they pressed on for six weeks.

Finally, with the help of the Underground Railroad, the family reached safety and freedom in Upper Canada. When Henson crossed the bridge over the Niagara River, he fell on his knees and kissed the ground.

Did You Know

The name "Underground Railroad" was inspired by the first steam-powered trains in North America. Brand new in the 1830s, trains were a quick and easy way to travel. They were just coming into use when Britain abolished slavery in Canada and all other colonies in 1834. Escaped enslaved people couldn't board real trains for fear of getting caught, but they rushed to board the Underground Railroad from that time on.

Passwords and Parcels

The conductors of the Underground Railroad communicated by means of secret passwords and signals — bird calls, special knocks and coded letters like this one:

"Dear Grinnell: Uncle Tom says if the roads are not too bad, you can look for those fleeces of wool by tomorrow. Send them on to test the market and price, no back charges …"

Those "fleeces of wool" were really escaped enslaved people hiding in a farm cart. Many other tricks were used to transport freedom-seekers. Some enslaved Black people hid in false-bottomed boxes. Others were shipped as freight on real trains. One enslaved man rode across the border stretched out in a coffin — knotholes in the wood gave him just enough air to breathe.

Disguises

Escaped enslaved people often wore disguises — makeup, wigs and moustaches all helped. Women would dress as men or men as women. Sometimes the freedom-seekers dressed up to look like prosperous free Black people living in a northern state — anything to confuse the slave catchers.

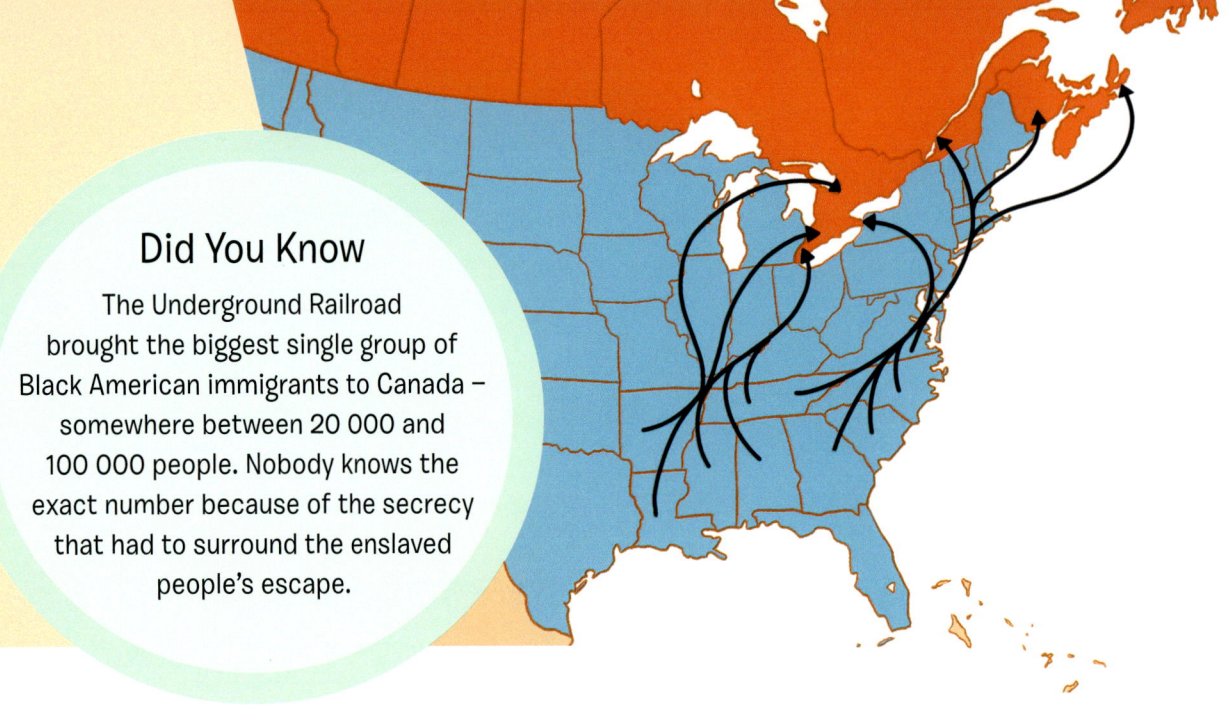

The Quakers

The Quakers (also called the Society of Friends), a Christian group in New England, were one of the first religious groups to oppose slavery. From the late 1700s on, the Quakers protested slavery and opened their homes to escaped enslaved people.

As the Underground Railroad grew, the Quakers became station masters and conductors. Levi Coffin was a Quaker and abolitionist who lived in Cincinnati, Ohio. He hid at least 100 enslaved Black people in his home every year and became the "president" of the Underground Railroad. In Canada, Quakers were always eager to help their Black neighbours.

Routes to Freedom

There were several routes that freedom-seekers could follow, but they were all dangerous. Men with vicious dogs hunted down escaped enslaved people for rewards. Many were recaptured, cruelly beaten and returned to the plantations they had escaped.

The escape routes led as directly as possible from slave-holding southern states, such as Tennessee and Mississippi, to free northern states or Canada. Large numbers of Black people crossed the Great Lakes into Upper Canada at towns such as Owen Sound, St. Catharines, Toronto and Windsor. Other routes led to the Maritime provinces.

Musical Codes

When they were on the plantations, the enslaved Black people had comforted themselves by composing and singing new songs. These spirituals – based on Bible stories – expressed their deep longing for their lost homes and their hopes that they would one day be free.

During the Underground Railroad, the words of the songs took on new meanings. One spiritual encouraged reluctant enslaved people to escape: "Get on board, little children, there's room for many a' more."

Another spiritual told freedom-seekers how to find their way to Canada: "Follow the Drinking Gourd." The enslaved people knew these were code words for the Big Dipper constellation. Why was that important? Because the two stars at the front of the Big Dipper's bowl point to the North Star, which guides travellers north.

Alexander Milton Ross, Conductor

Alexander Milton Ross was a white doctor from Belleville, Canada West (formerly Upper Canada, today Ontario), whose hobby was studying birds. Like many other people, he read *Uncle Tom's Cabin*, a novel by Harriet Beecher Stowe that depicted the cruelty of slavery. Ross decided to do all he could to help enslaved Black people escape.

Using his interest in birds as a cover, Ross made many trips to southern plantations. There, he would befriend the owners while secretly meeting the enslaved people. Ross gave the freedom-seekers clear maps of escape routes or guided them to Canada himself.

The End of the Underground Railroad

In 1865, after the North won the Civil War, slavery ended in the United States. Many Black people who had escaped to Canada returned home. Others remained and became Canadians. But for some years, they lived in fear of being kidnapped by slave catchers who ignored the law.

PROFILE : Harriet Tubman

The most famous conductor on the Underground Railroad was Harriet Tubman. She became known as her people's "Moses," after the biblical leader who led the Jews out of slavery in Egypt.

Born enslaved in 1820, Tubman was forced to do heavy work as a child. A head injury caused by an angry boss gave her narcolepsy for the rest of her life. (Narcolepsy causes a person to fall suddenly into a deep sleep.)

Tubman escaped from the plantation when she was about 30, using skills her father taught her – how to move silently through the forest, how to navigate by the stars and how to find plants to eat. But she couldn't bear to leave her family in slavery, so she returned and led them all to safety.

More than 300 enslaved Black people were guided to freedom by this dedicated conductor. Dressed as a man, Tubman would approach the slave quarters of a plantation and make her well-known owl-hoot signal. When the enslaved people heard it, they gathered their belongings and followed her.

Tubman was a strict leader. For the safety of the group, nobody was ever allowed to turn back. As a result, she could say proudly, "I never ran my train off its tracks, and I never lost a passenger."

Until 1858, Harriet Tubman's station on the Underground Railroad was in St. Catharines, Canada West. When the American Civil War broke out in 1861, she returned to the United States to work as a nurse, guide and spy for the northern side. Tubman is the only known woman who successfully carried out a rescue during the war – she freed 750 people.

Later, Tubman lived with her parents in Auburn, New York. She died in 1913, and her home is now a museum that honours her courage and extraordinary ability.

Life in Canada West

By 1850, there were as many as 60 000 free Black people in Canada West (formerly Upper Canada, today Ontario). The recent arrivals needed places to live, as well as jobs to support their families. In the countryside, the Dawn and Elgin Settlements offered schools, work and safe communities.

In Toronto, two enterprising Black men, T. F. Cary and R. B. Richards, opened the city's first ice house. They cut ice from mill ponds in winter and stored it, then sold and delivered it in the summer. Other men found work in hotels or with the new steam railroads. Some women took in laundry or sewing, or became maids in large houses.

The Dawn Settlement

In 1842, Josiah Henson helped establish an all-Black settlement called Dawn near Dresden, Canada West. Created by anti-slavery groups, it provided a new beginning for Black American refugees.

The Dawn Settlement boasted a brickyard, a grist mill for grinding grain and a sawmill. Settlers worked at one of these or farmed. The most important building was an industrial training school, one of the first in Canada. Over the next 30 years, the population grew to 500.

Josiah Henson in Canada West

With his new-found freedom, Josiah Henson helped many other enslaved people to escape. In 1841, he moved with his family to Dresden, then bought land in the Dawn Settlement. Over the years, Henson became Dawn's best-known resident and spokesman.

Henson told stories about his life to writer Harriet Beecher Stowe. He became the inspiration for the Uncle Tom character in Stowe's novel *Uncle Tom's Cabin*, published in 1852. This novel sold 300 000 copies in just its first year and helped raise awareness about the brutality of slavery. Henson also wrote a book about his own life. He travelled across North America and to England, meeting people and giving speeches.

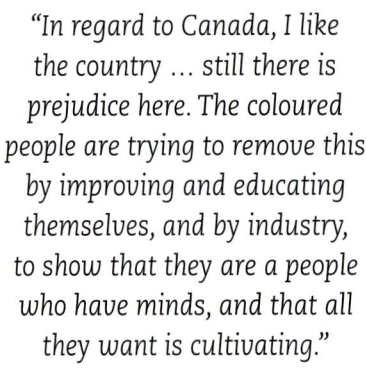

"In regard to Canada, I like the country … still there is prejudice here. The coloured people are trying to remove this by improving and educating themselves, and by industry, to show that they are a people who have minds, and that all they want is cultivating."

– Thomas Hedgebeth, Black man who fled North Carolina around 1850

The Elgin Settlement

The Elgin Settlement was the most successful early Black community in Canada West. It was the brainchild of Reverend William King, a white Presbyterian minister.

King opposed slavery, so he was troubled when his father-in-law left him 14 enslaved people in his will. He decided to start a community near Chatham, Canada West, where he could offer them freedom and a new life. Despite strong protests organized by nearby white people, King founded the Elgin Settlement in 1849.

PROFILE : Mary Ann Shadd

Black teacher and journalist Mary Ann Shadd was born in 1823 in Delaware, a free state. Shadd strongly believed that Black and white people should live together, not in separate communities such as Dawn and Elgin.

When Shadd moved to Canada in 1851, she set up a school in Windsor, Canada West, for those who had escaped slavery. She encouraged white children to attend, but many of their parents refused. To promote the cause of racial equality, Shadd started a newspaper called the *Provincial Freeman*, which came out strongly against slavery. Many Americans – Black and white – read Shadd's paper and learned of the Black Canadians' successes.

Shadd closed her school and returned to the United States in 1864 to recruit Black soldiers during the Civil War. Later, she attended law school at Howard University in Washington, D.C. As a lawyer, Shadd fought for many causes, including women's right to vote.

How Elgin Worked

King felt that former enslaved people needed three things: land, schools and churches. He sold new Black farmers 20 ha (50 acres) of land at a very low price. In return, they had to clear the fields, build houses and dig irrigation ditches.

By 1854, there were 300 families with large livestock herds, grain and tobacco farms, two sawmills and a brick-making company in Elgin. As property owners, Elgin residents had the right to vote.

Buxton Mission School

Buxton Mission School, opened in 1861, helped make Elgin successful. With support from the Presbyterian Church, it brought Black and white students together. The curriculum included reading, writing, math, religion, Greek and Latin. The school set very high standards for its students. Many Buxton graduates became community leaders, doctors, lawyers and teachers.

Today the school is part of the Buxton National Historic Site and Museum, which you can visit to find out more about the Elgin Settlement.

Did You Know

Mary Ann Shadd was the first Black woman in North America to start and run a newspaper, and the first woman to study for a law degree at an American university.

Back to the U.S.

During the 1850s — thanks to the Underground Railroad — about 60 000 Black people were living in Canadian provinces. In towns and on farms, newly free Black people were making decent lives for themselves. By contrast, their American cousins in the southern states were still enslaved.

The Black Canadian community was full of hope. But they had some worries, including how to get a good education for their children. Canada may have been the "promised land," but Black newcomers still encountered racism and prejudice in their new communities. Many schools in Canada didn't want Black students, or forced them to sit at the back of the classroom. After the American Civil War, this problem caused many Black people to return to the United States.

Segregated vs. Integrated Schools

In 1850, the Common Schools Act was passed in Canada West. This law allowed for the segregation of Black and white children into separate schools. A few years later, a similar law was passed in Nova Scotia. The all-Black schools that were built had little money. Often the buildings were second-rate and the teachers poorly paid. Still, many Black students succeeded despite these conditions.

Integrated schools such as Buxton School and Mary Ann Shadd's school, where Black and white children studied together, worked better. Many Black graduates from these schools went on to university and had successful careers.

The American Civil War

Black Canadians were distracted from their problems when the Civil War broke out in the United States in 1861. The abolition of slavery was a major goal of many of those fighting on the side of the anti-slavery states of the north against the pro-slavery states of the south. At first, Black Americans weren't allowed to fight. But Frederick Douglass, a famous Black abolitionist, got that changed.

Black Canadians wanted to fight against slavery, too. Josiah Henson, Mary Ann Shadd and Harriet Tubman returned to the United States to recruit Black soldiers. Thousands of Black Canadians joined the Union army of the northern states, and many died.

After the Civil War

The North won the Civil War. Across the South, homes, schools, farms and train tracks were destroyed. Newly freed enslaved people — 14 million of them — needed schooling and work. During a period called the Reconstruction, the American government tried to rebuild and find ways for Black and white people to live together after the horrors of slavery.

The Reconstruction Act of 1867 stated that "all persons born in the United States are citizens and have equal rights, and that all male citizens have the right to vote, regardless of race, colour or having been a slave."

A group called the Freedmen's Bureau set up hospitals and public schools for Black people across the southern states. And African Americans gained the right to buy land and enter politics.

The News Reaches Canada

After the Civil War, Canadian newspapers reported that slavery had ended in the United States. When Black Canadians learned about the improvements being made to benefit former enslaved people, including well-funded public schools being set up in the South, it made them think. Should they stay in Canada or go back to the United States?

Goodbye, Canada

The pull to return to the United States was strong. In Canada, Black people were having a hard time finding good jobs. Many wanted to reunite with family and friends. White Canadians did little to stop them from leaving. Some felt that Black people should return to the United States, and others wanted to stop any more Black refugees from coming to Canada.

Over the next 30 years, about two-thirds of the Black people in Canada returned to the United States, hoping for a better life. Canada's Black population declined from 60 000 to 18 000.

Did You Know

In 1857, Dr. Anderson Ruffin Abbott became the first Black graduate of Toronto's Medical College. He served as a surgeon for the Union army during the Civil War, then returned to Canada.

The Civil War

- The Civil War began in 1861 and ended in 1865.
- The war was fought between the northern (Union) states and the southern (Confederate) states.
- The Confederacy wanted to be an independent country and to continue slavery.
- In 1863, President Abraham Lincoln passed the Emancipation Proclamation, which freed all enslaved people.
- In 1865, the Union won the war, and the end of slavery was confirmed.

Issue: Prejudice and Racism

Understanding the history of Black Canadians means understanding prejudice and racism. Black people in Canada have always faced hardship because of the prejudices of white society.

Prejudice means having an opinion, usually negative, about someone before you have met them or learned much about them. It can also mean having an opinion about a whole race of people, even though you know very little about that race.

Racism is the belief that people's traits and abilities are determined by their race and that one race is better than another. This prejudice can make people treat other races badly. Racism can be individual — everything from verbal insults to physical violence — or institutional. Institutional racism describes systems that harm a particular racial group, such as segregated schools for Black children or laws that allow landlords to refuse to rent homes to someone because of their race.

Prejudice and Racism in Everyday Life

An example of a racial stereotype is "All Black people are good at sports." Of course, it's not a bad thing to be good at sports. But this kind of stereotyping can lead to prejudice. When the statement gets repeated often, it can make people forget that Black people are also excellent businesspeople, lawyers, teachers, writers and many other things.

An example of a racist act is spray-painting hateful slogans on a Black church or beating up people of another race because they're different from you. Extreme racist acts are also called hate crimes.

Did You Know

Around the world, legal or formal systems that kept Black and white people apart were called segregation (U.S.) or apartheid (South Africa). In Canada, segregation wasn't an official national policy, but it still occurred in many communities.

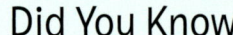

The Roots of Racism

Throughout history, Black people have arrived in Canada in waves — Black Loyalists, Jamaican Maroons, refugees from the War of 1812, passengers on the Underground Railroad. Each immigrant group arrived weary from fierce battles or treacherous journeys, but eager to start new lives.

However, other Canadian settlers often discriminated against Black immigrants. Darker skin made the newcomers look distinct, and many settlers associated Black people with slavery and viewed them as inferior. Also, few former enslaved people could read or write because southern U.S. laws had forbidden their education.

A History of Prejudice

In the Maritimes, the Black Loyalists struggled to scratch out a living. Along with the Jamaican Maroons, many eventually left to look for a better life in Sierra Leone. Later, the refugees from the War of 1812 faced similar problems.

The freedom-seekers who escaped to Upper Canada via the Underground Railroad were also poorly treated by the government and white people in their communities. As a solution, many Black people formed their own communities, with separate schools and churches.

Racism Is Wrong

Prejudice and racism rob all people of something valuable. Young people who experience racism in school or in the community may lose confidence in themselves and their future. Racism affects more than a person's sense of self – it can impact their mental and physical health and their ability to get a job, find a home and build a comfortable life.

Nobody can tell by looking at a stranger how that person will behave or what she may achieve. Racist attitudes make it impossible for people to appreciate everyone in their community and share their contributions.

Learning from History

Black history shows that Canadian society has discriminated against Black people because of their race. More importantly, it reveals the valuable contributions Black people have made in Canada. As people learn more about these contributions, prejudice and racism may diminish. Perhaps then, Black Canadians may fully enjoy their right to live as equals with other Canadians.

PROFILE : Viola Desmond

On November 8, 1946, Viola Desmond went to a movie at the Roseland Theatre in New Glasgow, Nova Scotia. She was sold a ticket to the second-rate balcony seats. That's where Black people were expected to sit in those days, not just in Nova Scotia but across Canada.

However, Desmond sat downstairs in the better seats. When she refused to move, the police were called and Desmond was arrested and jailed overnight.

Charged with failing to pay a 19-cent extra tax for her downstairs ticket, she was fined $20 and sentenced to 30 days in prison. Fortunately, the Nova Scotia Association for the Advancement of Coloured People, and other friends, helped her win her appeal. Newspapers like the *Clarion* (see Carrie Best on page 57) reported on Desmond's story, and the publicity helped to put an end to this discrimination.

Desmond showed great courage in standing up for her rights. But she was just an ordinary person who represented how many other Black Canadians were feeling about the racism they experienced.

West Coast Adventures

Before the American Civil War, a group of Black Californians were thinking about moving north. Until 1858, they'd been living freely in California. But the new state governor wanted to force African Americans to pay a fee to live in California — and to wear a badge showing they'd paid it. He also allowed an escaped enslaved person to be captured on Californian soil.

Then Black Californians received a message from Vancouver Island, Britain's first colony on the West Coast. Governor James Douglas wanted people to come and set up sawmills, mines and salmon fishing operations. He was especially eager to attract educated, hard-working settlers, such as the Black Californians, who would be loyal to Britain.

So Governor Douglas, a fur trader whose mother had African ancestry, invited the Black Californians to come and see the new colony.

The Governor's Promise

Governor Douglas made these promises to the Black Californians:

- They could buy land for $5 per 0.4 ha (1 acre).
- They would pay no land taxes for two years.
- After they had owned land for nine months, they could vote and serve as jury members.
- After seven years, they could receive full citizenship rights as British subjects.

In return for Governor Douglas's guarantees, the Black Californians were to promise to defend the young colony. Pleased with these arrangements, the Californians encouraged the rest of their community to join them. In April 1858, 400 Black Californian families travelled from San Francisco to Victoria, the colony's most important town. Vancouver Island remained a welcoming place for Black people until Governor Douglas retired in 1864.

Life on Vancouver Island

The Black Californians were determined to succeed on Vancouver Island. Most stayed in Victoria and opened new businesses. The finest restaurant in Victoria, Ringo's, and the best barbershop were both owned by Black businessmen.

John Sullivan Deas was another successful Black entrepreneur. Trained as a tinsmith, he took over a salmon canning factory on the Fraser River and shipped thousands of cases of salmon to Britain every year.

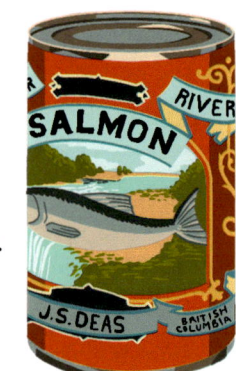

Mifflin Gibbs

The first Black politician in Canada, Mifflin Gibbs, was elected to Victoria City Council in 1867. A good businessman, Gibbs ran a general store that competed with the Hudson's Bay Company and also built a coal mine and a railway in the Queen Charlotte Islands (now called Haida Gwaii). In 1868, Gibbs was a delegate at the convention that decided that British Columbia would become part of Canada.

Gold Rush

In 1858, gold was discovered in the Fraser River on the British Columbia mainland. By year's end, 20 000 prospectors had passed through Victoria in search of gold. Governor Douglas was worried that these gold seekers, most of them Americans, might try to claim the territory for the United States. Just in case, he enforced stern justice in the wild new mining towns. He knew that, if necessary, he could count on the loyal support of the Black Californians.

Did You Know

In 1860, the Black Californians formed the Victoria Pioneer Rifle Company to guard Vancouver Island against any American attack.

"I was one of the successful gold prospectors in British Columbia, although there were 10 years of doubt when I never made a single strike! … I was not one to give up and I'm glad I kept trying … In 1884 we found several gold-bearing streams around Lorne Creek. I understand that one of the streams was later called McDame."

– Henry McDame, Black prospector

PROFILE : Sylvia Stark

Sylvia Stark was one of British Columbia's first pioneers. Born into slavery in Missouri in 1839, she learned to read by watching white children do their lessons. When she was 10, her father bought freedom for the family, and in 1851 they moved to California.

Sylvia married Louis Stark and had two children. When California introduced restrictions against Black people, the family fled north, arriving on Saltspring Island (near Vancouver Island) in 1860. Their 15 dairy cows were lowered into the water by ropes so they could swim ashore.

While Louis ran the farm, Sylvia had two more children and became a volunteer midwife and nurse. Years later, the Starks survived a smallpox epidemic, then moved to the Nanaimo area. But Sylvia missed Saltspring. She returned to the island, where she died at age 106.

Cowboys and Pioneers

In 1867, the Dominion of Canada was created when Canada East (Quebec), Canada West (Ontario), New Brunswick and Nova Scotia joined together. The Canadian government quickly realized that the country would be much stronger if it was bigger. But how should it expand?

The government soon began to look west. It saw buffalo herds still roaming on endless grassland stretching west to the mountains. The Cree and other Indigenous Peoples had been living on the land and hunting for game for generations. But the government wanted pioneers to settle down and farm the land instead. It also planned to push the Canadian Pacific Railway all the way west to expand Canada from coast to coast.

"The Last Best West"

In the 1890s, Canada began to advertise cheap land in the Prairies to attract settlers from Europe and the United States. Among those tempted to take up this offer were African Americans living in the midwestern states.

To Black people who weren't firmly settled by 1905, Canadian railway and government posters looked very attractive. They had headlines such as "The Last Best West," and they advertised land at $2 per 0.4 ha (1 acre) in Saskatchewan — the price in the neighbouring state of North Dakota was $50.

Black Canadian Pioneers

Between 1905 and 1909, many hundreds of Black Americans journeyed north from their homes to the Canadian Prairies. Most travelled by train and arrived at small border towns in Manitoba and Saskatchewan. Some of the immigrants chose to make their homes in those provinces.

But the majority of Black Americans journeyed west to Alberta. Some went to booming cities such as Edmonton. Others decided to live in rural areas as cowboys or homesteaders.

Homesteading

When the Black pioneers arrived in the Prairies, they found land covered with trees and underbrush. It took weeks to clear, especially because they often had to work without horses or oxen. A pioneer's first house was usually a log cabin with a sod (grass and earth) roof. Neighbours — whether Black or white — helped one another build their homes. The pioneers planted large gardens and hunted for fresh meat such as deer, duck, pheasant and rabbit.

Working in Winter Weather

Some Black homesteaders took on extra work during the winter. They hauled heavy loads by sleigh to northern settlements such as Fort McMurray, Alberta, where the railroad didn't reach.

There were no inns where they could sleep. To keep warm at night, they'd scoop out snow from a snowbank, lay down spruce boughs to make a sleeping mat, then pile more snow over their blankets.

A few years later, when the Canadian government wanted to restrict Black immigration, it made ridiculous claims, including that Black people weren't suited to Canada's cold climate. Brave Black homesteaders had already proved how wrong that was!

Surviving in a Cold Climate

How did Black settlers from southern climates manage to survive in the frozen north? Take a look at life in a small community north of Edmonton, Alberta. In the early 1900s, Amber Valley was the largest rural Black settlement in western Canada.

One of its first settlers, Martha Edwards, lived with her husband, Jeff, in her father's log cabin. There was no bathtub or toilet. The wind howled through cracks in the walls. But Martha says they made do by stuffing the cracks with rags and loading up on warm bedding and firewood. For Christmas, the family ate prairie chicken (grouse) and moose meat, instead of turkey.

These Black settlers learned how to survive in Canada's cold climate very well. The children, grandchildren and great-grandchildren of hardy pioneer families such as the Edwards family still live in the Amber Valley area.

PROFILE : John Ware

John Ware was born enslaved in the United States, but he was freed at the end of the Civil War. He became a cowboy in Texas, then moved to Alberta in 1882.

Tall and powerful, Ware knew all about handling horses and throwing a lasso. He became a famous rodeo cowboy who could wrestle a steer to the ground. One story tells how he rode over a cliff into a river while trying to tame a bucking horse. The spectators were amazed when Ware and the horse came up alive, with Ware still in the saddle!

John Ware married Mildred Lewis after he came to Canada, and together they raised five children and ran a successful ranch. Ware died in 1905, when his horse stumbled in a hole, fell and crushed him.

Today you can visit the John Ware Historic Cabin in Dinosaur Provincial Park near Calgary, Alberta.

The Exodusters

By the 1880s, the promise of a good life for former enslaved people in the United States was over. In the South, violent anti-Black groups such as the Ku Klux Klan had formed, and new laws forced the segregation of Black and white people.

Fifty thousand Black Americans escaped by heading west to new states such as Oklahoma. Many poor farm labourers — known as Exodusters — went to take up offers of free land. Many Exodusters did well in Oklahoma, creating large cattle ranches. But some farmers were hit by drought and floods, and others found that land was becoming too expensive. They began to think about moving to Canada.

Did You Know

The name "Exodusters" comes from the book of Exodus in the Bible, which tells the story of the Israelites' flight from slavery in Egypt. "Exodus" means the departure of a large group of people, and "dusters" refers to the dry soil of Oklahoma.

Trouble in Oklahoma

By 1910, things were getting worse for the Exodusters in Oklahoma. The state had passed segregation laws like the ones in the southern states. More and more Black families looked toward Canada as a refuge from prejudice and violence.

A group of Black people travelled to the Canadian Prairies to investigate. One of them was Henry Sneed, a former Texan, who liked what he saw. When he returned to Oklahoma, Sneed helped to organize a large group of Exodusters who had decided to emigrate to Canada. Knowing Canada's record, they were sure they would be welcomed.

Protests from White Canadians

Up until 1911, under Prime Minister Sir Wilfrid Laurier, Canada had actively recruited Black settlers to the Prairies. Now, anti-Black racism was starting to build. Newspapers ran stories about problems that sprang up when large numbers of Black people moved to northern American cities. But the papers didn't report on Black people's success stories.

When white Canadians heard rumours that a large group of Exodusters was planning to come north, many called for an end to Black immigration.

Canada, Here We Come!

The Exodusters had faced discouragement before and won. Encouraged by Henry Sneed's report on Canada, a group of about 190 Black people from Oklahoma and Kansas made the trek north in 1911. They filled nine railway cars with horses and farming tools.

At the Canadian border, officials tried to stump the Exodusters with health and citizenship tests. But because the group had money, property and good health, they passed easily. They went on to establish communities from western Alberta to Thunder Bay, Ontario. Between 1909 and 1911, about 1500 Exodusters emigrated from Oklahoma to the Canadian Prairies.

Stopping Black Immigration

Still worried by western protests, Laurier's government tried to pass regulation to stop Black immigration for one year — from 1911 to 1912. It stated that Black people were "unsuitable to the climate and requirements of Canada."

Although the regulation never became law, Black people got the message that they were no longer welcome in Canada. In fact, Black immigration to Canada sharply declined from 1912 until the 1950s.

Discouragement from Canada

Faced with protests from white Canadians, Prime Minister Laurier came up with new ideas to discourage Exodusters from coming to Canada.

One government scheme sent Dr. G. W. Miller, a Black doctor from Chicago, to hold meetings in Oklahoma, Kansas and other western states. In his speeches, Dr. Miller tried to convince hopeful farmers that they would perish in Canada's waist-high snows. The ground was frozen year-round, he said, so they wouldn't be able to farm it.

The government also instructed officials at the border to make Black Americans answer tough questions about their health and character. The idea was that they would fail the test and be sent back home.

PROFILE : Mattie Mayes

Mattie Mayes was a successful Oklahoman immigrant. In 1910, when she was 60-years-old, she and her husband, Joe, travelled by train to Canada with 13 children and grandchildren and 10 other families.

The group chose to homestead in Eldon, not far from North Battleford, Saskatchewan. After 10 years of their hard work, Mattie's farm was doing well. The community built a Baptist church, and Joe became the first preacher. A few years later, they built a school.

Mattie was a warm and caring leader in the community until she died in 1953 at age 103. Her descendants include Reuben Mayes, the great NFL football player, and Lesa Stringer, who's been a member of Canada's national women's bobsleigh team.

CANADA WILL BAR THE NEGRO OUT

Official Notice Given by Dominion to United States Consul

UNFITTED FOR HEALTHY CLIMATE

The Action of Dominion Leading to Conference in Washington

Washington, D.C., April 26. — The plans of the Dominion of Canada to adopt restrictions against the entering of their country by American negroes was the subject of a conference today between Assistant Secretary of State Wilson and John K. Jones, consul general of the U.S. at Winnipeg. Mr. Jones presented a recommendation from the Canadian immigration authorities indicating that the American negro may be barred on the ground that he could not become adapted to the rigorous northern climate and consequently might become a public charge. Such action is authorized by the immigration act of Canada.

Working for Respect

Until World War II, Black Canadian men and women were kept out of many jobs and professions. They couldn't attend nursing schools or teachers' colleges, join hockey leagues or belong to trade unions. Only the lowest-paying jobs were open to them.

In cities such as Halifax and Toronto, 80% of Black women worked as domestic servants in white Canadian homes. Many men worked for the railway as porters. But these jobs often didn't allow for promotion to better positions.

A Sense of Community

Travelling from coast to coast, porters kept in touch with Black people across the country. In Winnipeg, the men got together at Haynes Chicken Shack. This famous restaurant was owned by Piercy Haynes, a railway worker, boxer and jazz pianist.

While their husbands were away working on the railways, some Black women in Toronto formed the Eureka Friendly Club. They met every other Thursday afternoon to share a meal and listen to music. A favourite song was "Some of These Days," written by the African Canadian Shelton Brooks.

Work as a Domestic Servant

Domestic servants spent the day cleaning their employer's house, caring for the children and sometimes cooking meals. These Black women were lucky if their employer was kind. Then in the evening, the women had to go home and do the same work for their own families.

The pay was poor and, because they worked alone, it was hard for the women to band together and demand better conditions. Most women were paid less than men, even for the same work.

Work as a Railway Porter

Starting in the early 1900s, large numbers of Black men were hired as railway porters. Porters carried suitcases for passengers, shined shoes and made up beds in the overnight sleeping cars.

Being a porter was one of the few steady jobs Black men could get at that time. So they came to Montreal (where the hiring was done) from across Canada, the United States and the Caribbean islands, wanting to work for Canadian Pacific Railway and Canadian National Railways.

Porters' wages were low, but the men could earn good tips. Still, they had to endure racist remarks from some white passengers, and they were separated from their families for days and weeks at a time.

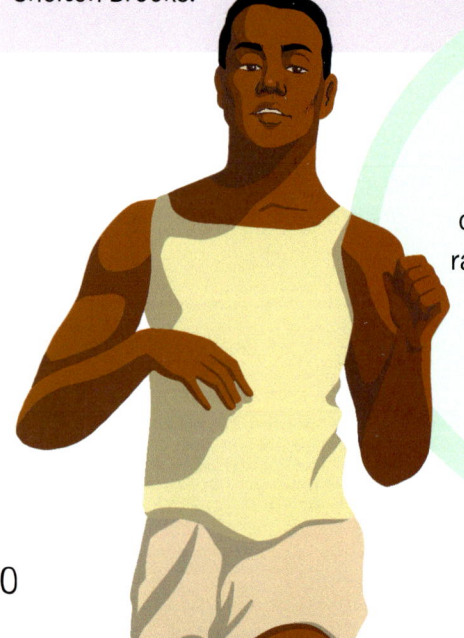

Did You Know

Ray Lewis of Hamilton, Ontario, was a porter who was also a world-class athlete. Lewis not only trained hard, but he had to overcome racial insults while working on the railway. In 1932, Lewis brought home a bronze medal as part of the 4 x 400 relay team at the Los Angeles Olympics. In 2001, Lewis received the Order of Canada, the highest honour awarded to a person by the Government of Canada.

The Brotherhood of Sleeping Car Porters

In 1917, Black porters formed a union — an organization to help them fight for better jobs. This union, the Order of Sleeping Car Porters, was the first in Canada to allow Black members. But the union only managed to make a few improvements to working conditions.

After World War II, the president of the American union the Brotherhood of Sleeping Car Porters helped the porters set up branches of the BSCP in Canada. By 1955, thanks to the support of this new union, the Canadian porters had won their struggle. From then on, a Black porter could be promoted to dining-car waiter or conductor.

Hard-Won Respect

In 1944, Ontario became the first province to pass an act to prevent discrimination against any person because of race or religion. Other provinces soon followed.

When Black Canadian men were fighting in World War II, women took over their jobs in factories and other workplaces. Many Black women liked these jobs better than domestic service. But when the men came home to Canada, they wanted their jobs back. Some Black women returned to domestic service, but many upgraded their education, found new job opportunities and fought for racial equality and women's rights.

Railway porters continued to improve their working conditions. Through their efforts, the porters created new and better opportunities for Black people in Canada.

PROFILE : Stanley G. Grizzle

Born in Toronto in 1918, Stanley G. Grizzle was a railway porter who became president of the Toronto branch of the Brotherhood of Sleeping Car Porters. He spent the 1950s campaigning for equal rights for Black people.

Grizzle was the first Black judge in Ontario's Citizenship Court and the first Black Canadian to run for election to the Ontario legislature. In recognition of his distinguished service, he received the Order of Canada in 1995.

Fighting in Two World Wars

In the 1900s, Canada fought in two world wars. Twice, Canadian soldiers, sailors and fliers went overseas to help defend Britain and its Allies.

Black Canadians wanted to show their loyalty to Britain and also help Canada — still a young country — come together as a nation.

Black Canadians also knew that, in order to be treated equally with white Canadians, they needed to accept the dangers of war. But serving their country proved to be difficult.

Nova Scotia No. 2 Construction Battalion

In 1916, an all-Black unit of 600 men called the No. 2 Construction Battalion was formed. It took almost two years of protesting and lobbying by Black Canadians to form the battalion. They weren't allowed to fight, but they cut lumber in France, built huts for soldiers at the battlefronts and dug trenches.

Training took place in both Pictou and Truro, Nova Scotia, where the battalion formed its own brass band to lead marches. In 1917, the men sailed across the Atlantic Ocean, always under threat from enemy submarines. Among the soldiers were the sons of cowboy John Ware.

The battalion's first head-quarters, in Pictou, Nova Scotia, is now a National Historic Site. In 2022, the Canadian government apologized to the descendants of the No. 2 Construction Battalion for the mistreatment the men received during and after the war.

World War I

On August 4, 1914, Germany, under its leader, Kaiser Wilhelm II, invaded Belgium. That same day, Britain declared war on Germany and its empire. All the countries of the British Empire, including Canada, sent troops to fight on the battlefields of France.

Black Canadians lined up at recruitment offices to volunteer for service. But thousands were turned away. Some white officers said that Black and white soldiers shouldn't mix. Black Canadian leaders, newspaper reporters and clergymen protested strongly, and by 1915 a few Black soldiers were allowed to join white regiments.

On the Home Front

Black Canadians formed patriotic clubs that raised money to support the war effort. Men volunteered to work on farms and in factories and hospitals. In Vancouver, women formed a branch of the Universal Black Cross nurses to care for wounded Black servicemen.

"Do not let any man tell you different, no man is any braver than a Black man … After all, the Black man went over there, he trained like a soldier, he fought like a soldier and he died like a soldier, and that is all any white man can do."

– Sergeant A. Seymour Tyler, Black Canadian World War II veteran

Between the Wars

World War I was a time of pride and sorrow for Black Canadians. They were proud of their war efforts, but by the time the war ended in 1918, many Black soldiers were wounded or dead. Black Canadians hoped that their wartime service would lead to better relations between the races at home.

In 1919, Black American Marcus Garvey, who was born in Jamaica, opened branches of his Universal Negro Improvement Association in Canada. Its goal was to empower and unite Black people by helping them get better jobs and work for their rights. The organization also encouraged Black people to return to Africa.

Black Canadians were becoming more aware of their heritage. In the 1920s, Montreal, with its many jazz clubs, became a lively centre of Black culture. Black Canadians were full of hope for their future.

But in the 1930s, the Depression brought poverty and hard times across Canada. However, it also helped improve race relations by bringing people together. No matter what their skin colour, most people were desperately poor and needed to help one another to survive.

PROFILE : The Carty Brothers

The Carty family of Saint John, New Brunswick, sent seven sons to World War II. Adolphus, William, Clyde, Donald and Gerald Carty all enlisted in the air force, while Robert and Malcolm joined the army. The brothers fought hard for their country, and at the close of the war, all seven were discharged with high rank.

World War II

World War II broke out in 1939. Germany, led by Adolf Hitler and the Nazi Party, invaded Czechoslovakia (now two countries: Czechia and Slovakia) and Poland. Britain, Canada and the Allies declared war, vowing to stop Hitler.

In this war, Black Canadians had an easier time enlisting in the army, navy and air force. They refused to serve in segregated units like the Construction Battalion. Instead, they fought in racially mixed units and helped Britain and its Allies win the war in 1945.

On the home front, Black women were allowed to work in weapons factories. For most of them, it was their first chance to escape from domestic work such as child-minding and housekeeping.

After the Wars

Black Canadians' participation in two world wars led to better race relations. White Canadians realized that Black sons and daughters — just like their own children — had given their lives for their country. As well, returning Black soldiers would not tolerate the discrimination of the past. Many Black and white Canadians found a new determination to build a more just society.

Did You Know

The first Black person and one of the first Canadians honoured with the Victoria Cross, the British Empire's highest award for bravery, was Naval Quartermaster William Hall in 1857.

Caribbean and African Immigrants

Canada is often called a country of immigrants. But Canada hasn't always welcomed everybody who wants to immigrate here.

During the first half of the 1900s, Canada encouraged white people from the United States and certain European countries to come. They were known as the "preferred nationalities." Black people, Asians and many other racial and ethnic groups were discouraged and even prevented from immigrating.

But after World War II, Canadian immigration policy began to change, thanks in large part to Black activists such as Harry Gairey and Donald Moore. They helped open the door for Black immigrants from the Caribbean, Guyana (South America) and Africa.

Changing the Immigration Act

In 1954, a group of 35 Black Canadian activists met with federal Cabinet ministers (advisers to the prime minister) in Ottawa. The group wanted to change the Immigration Act of 1952 because it discriminated against people of colour. One of the group's leaders, Donald Moore, reminded the Cabinet ministers of Black Canadians' heroic service in the world wars.

After years of pressure, the government passed a new Immigration Act in 1962. Would-be immigrants could no longer be discriminated against because of their race or religion.

The West Indian Domestic Scheme

In 1955, the government took a first step in opening up Black immigration. The Domestic Scheme encouraged Caribbean women to come to Canada, but only if they promised to work as domestic servants for one year. Many women took the opportunity — 2700 over the next 10 years. Often they left behind husbands and children.

After their year of domestic service, many women enrolled in university or worked as teachers, nurses and office workers. Later, they brought their families to Canada.

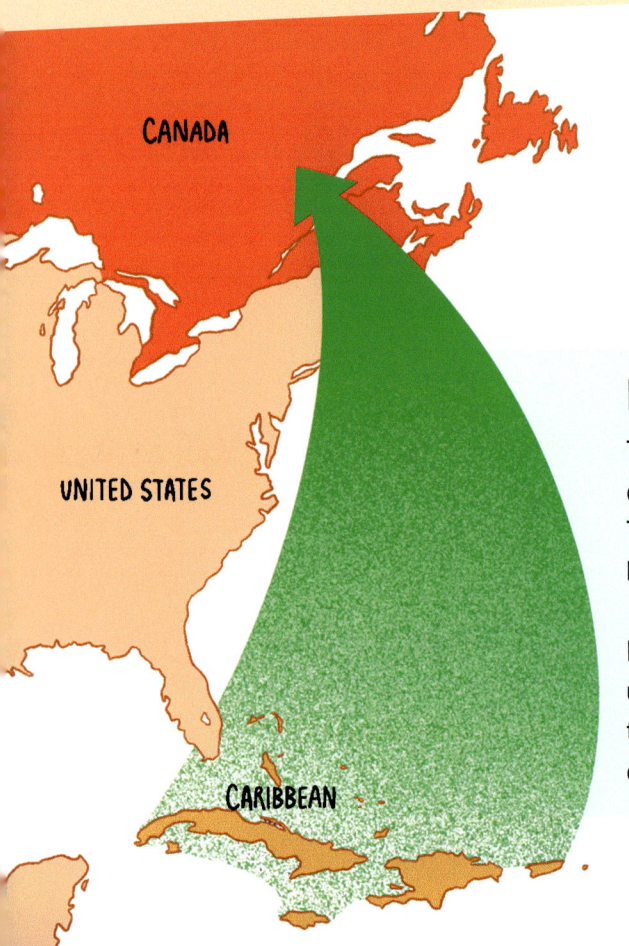

CANADA

UNITED STATES

CARIBBEAN

Blue Skies, Tropical Seas

The Caribbean, also called the West Indies, is a chain of island countries including Barbados, Jamaica, St. Lucia and Trinidad and Tobago. The tropical climate brings hot sunshine, rainy seasons and hurricanes.

Most Caribbean people are of African descent. For centuries, European countries operated sugar plantations in the Caribbean using slave labour. By the 1960s, most of these countries had gained their independence. But the impacts of slavery and colonialism continued – many people remained poor or had trouble finding jobs.

The Points System

Canada still needed a better way than the Immigration Act of 1962 and the Domestic Scheme to decide who would be allowed to immigrate. In 1967, a method called the points system was introduced. People who wished to immigrate were awarded points for such things as education, job skills and ability to speak English or French. Anyone who obtained at least 70 points out of 100 was allowed to immigrate. Now the criteria were the same for hopeful immigrants from all countries.

Under the points system, many Caribbean people were well qualified to immigrate. During the 1970s and 1980s, 315 000 immigrated to Canada, mostly from Jamaica, Trinidad and Tobago and Haiti.

They settled mainly in the cities. English-speaking people found jobs in Toronto or other cities across the country where English was the main language. French-speaking Haitians moved to Montreal.

Black African Immigrants

Beginning in 1980, more Black immigrants came to Canada directly from Africa. They hailed from many different countries, including Ghana, Nigeria, Ethiopia, Sierra Leone, Somalia and South Africa. Some were economic immigrants seeking new jobs and opportunities, and some were refugees from famine and war.

Adjusting to Canada

Some Caribbean and African immigrants had problems adjusting to Canada. The winters felt bitterly cold. Fathers or mothers who came on their own were lonely until they could bring their families. They had to get used to new customs and different ways of speaking. Even those who had immigrated first to Britain and then to Canada found the adjustment difficult.

Black people were the majority in their home countries, but in Canada, they stood out in the sea of white faces. Their children had to adjust to a different school system. And the new immigrants didn't always feel welcomed by their white Canadian neighbours.

Community Support

Black Canadians already settled here were eager to help the newcomers. They worked together to offer young people dance, drama and music programs, as well as academic scholarships. Carnival festivals, concerts and picnics were some of the traditions they continued.

Like other Black Canadians, Caribbean and African immigrants entered politics, started businesses and wrote books. They became involved in already-established magazines and newspapers, such as *Contrast*, for the community.

Waves of Black Immigration to Canada

1783   Black Loyalists

1796   Jamaican Maroons

1814   Refugees of the War of 1812

1831–1865 Underground Railroad

1858   Black Californians

1911   Oklahoma Exodusters

1955   Caribbean Domestic Service Workers

1967   Caribbean Immigrants, from the Caribbean and from England

1980   African Immigrants

Unequal Treatment and Activism

Black people entered Canada at many different times in history to be free, but their rights and privileges were not complete or automatic. Biased ideas about Black people led to discrimination and marginalization that left many Black people with less than others.

As society has modernized, it has become unacceptable to exclude racial groups from housing, education or jobs. But it took the protests and advocacy of members of the Black community, sometimes with the support of non-Black allies, to press their message and secure the changes that make things better for us all.

Settlements and Housing

In the 1700s through to the early 1900s, Black people were encouraged to live in areas that were not suited for farming or that were far from other types of work. People cleared their land, built homes and communities but found they were denied the full ownership of their property. Many Black settlements scattered across Nova Scotia, New Brunswick, Alberta and Ontario were abandoned because they were on such barren land. Both the Bog of Prince Edward Island and Hogan's Alley in Vancouver were lost to urban development.

Recognition for Africville

When Africville, a community near Halifax, was classified as a slum, it was torn down and residents were forced to leave despite community protest. This happened even though residents paid taxes that could have funded improvements to the community. The Carvery brothers, Irvine and Eddie, protested the removal and destruction of Africville for decades. Irvine was the president of the Africville Genealogy Society and wrote a book on the community, while Eddie built a protest site on the land. The City of Halifax eventually issued an apology to the former residents and a replica of Seaview Baptist Church was created. (For more on Africville, see page 54.)

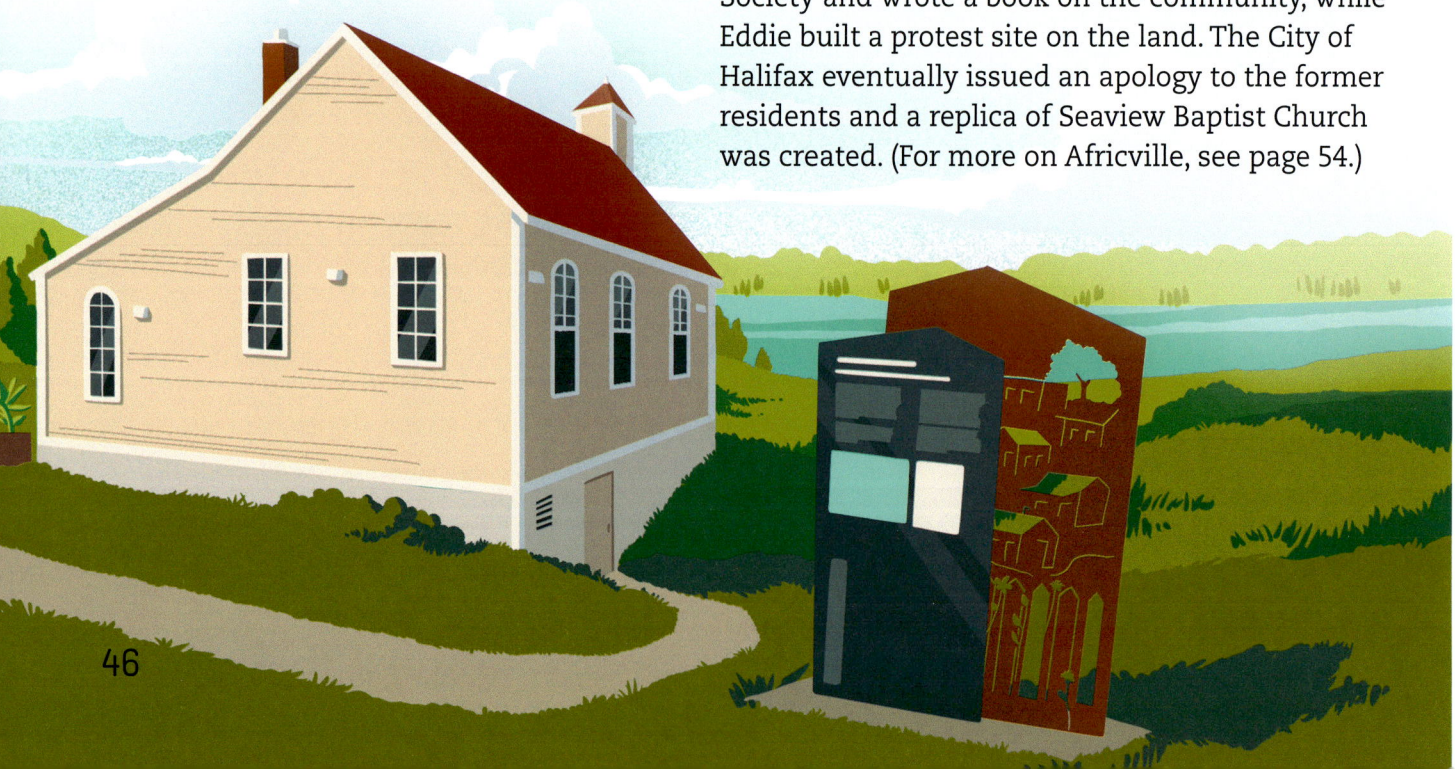

Segregated Education

With the arrival of freedom-seeking Black people in the 1850s, many communities passed laws that created separate schools along racial and religious lines. The last segregated Black school in Canada was closed in 1965. Official and unofficial segregation also existed in medical and legal schools and teachers' colleges until the 1960s, forcing those who could afford to do so to head to the U.S. for training.

Did You Know

Ontario MPP Leonard Braithwaite, who became the first Black Canadian elected to a provincial legislature in 1963, spoke out against segregated schools and ensured their closure.

Black History in Schools

For decades, advocates have campaigned for Black history to be taught in schools and demanded that Black students be treated equitably. Today, Black Canadian history has become part of the curriculum in many provinces, but it's still seen as optional. But students, teachers and advocates are speaking out. In 2021, three Mississauga students used social media and the momentum of the 2020 Black Lives Matter protests to get the course called "A History of Black People in Canada" added to their high school curriculum!

Labour Force Discrimination

Into the 1900s, Black people were denied entry to professional schools and trade unions. Many secured training in the United States or Britain, but returned to find they were still being discriminated against in hiring. To survive, they took whatever jobs they could find, often abandoning their dreams. By becoming more vocal, joining forces and organizing stronger protests against mistreatment, Black people changed hiring practices and admission policies for schools and unions.

PROFILE : Hugh Burnett

After risking his life defending Canada during World War II, Hugh Burnett was shocked to find that he would still not be served in restaurants in his hometown of Dresden, Ontario. In 1948, Burnett formed the National Unity Association (NUA) to campaign for racial equality and an end to discrimination. NUA's efforts led to Ontario's Fair Employment Practices Act (1951) and Fair Accommodation Practices Act (1954), which outlawed discrimination in employment, public services and housing. Burnett's work, along with these laws, paved the way for more human rights legislation in Ontario and Canada.

Organizing for Change

The railway porters' activism in 1917 and beyond led to unionized work. Hugh Burnett and the NUA created the basis for new human rights laws in Ontario and Canada between 1948 and 1956. In the late 1980s, the Coalition of Black Trade Unionists (Ontario) organized to address the economic and employment concerns of their members. And in 2020, Black federal government workers launched a class action lawsuit with charges of denied promotions and few salary increases for Black employees. History shows us that fighting against inequitable treatment can improve things for everyone.

The Fight Continues

What you've read about African and Black history in Canada will help you to understand how things are today. The prejudice and discrimination that Black people still experience are connected to views, myths and actions related to the Atlantic slave trade and Canada's 200-year history of slavery.

What do you do when you know something is not right? Think about the Underground Railroad, the first freedom movement in North America. At that time, it was legal to enslave people, but many did not support that practice and fought against it. However, once Black people were "free," they were still denied real equality and inclusion.

Fighting for Our Rights

Even when rights are gained, they can be lost through changes in government and society or threatened by the harmful actions of individuals and groups. Acquiring and maintaining rights and freedoms requires constant attention. People like Viola Desmond, Hugh Burnett and Donald Moore fought for greater freedoms and rights for Black people here in Canada.

So, what do you do when the world is watching? When the law does not seem to be working as it should? How do you make sure these wrongs do not happen again?

Starting a Movement

Protests are one way to draw attention to inequality and seek solutions to laws and events that are unjust. Protesting can be writing a letter to a politician, or signing or even creating a petition. Some protests involve gathering large numbers of people together through strikes, marches and rallies. Labour, environmental and civil rights activists have used these methods to bring about changes for society. Today, Black activists and allies continue to create protest movements such as Black Lives Matter.

Black Lives Matter

Black Lives Matter began as an online social movement in July 2013 after a Hispanic man from Florida, George Zimmerman, was acquitted of killing unarmed Black teenager Trayvon Martin. In response to the acquittal, three activists in the U.S. — Alicia Garza, Opal Tometi and Patrisse Cullors — created the hashtag #BlackLivesMatter (#BLM). It launched a global social justice movement. People protested, demonstrated and shared their experiences of anti-Black racism while seeking change.

In Canada, a Black Lives Matter chapter was founded in 2014 by Sandy Hudson and Rodney Diverlus in response to the police killings of Jermaine Carby in Brampton, Ontario, and Michael Brown in St. Louis, Missouri, and to general police violence.

PROFILE : Desmond Cole

Toronto's Desmond Cole, a journalist, activist and author of *The Skin We're In: A Year of Black Resistance and Power*, raised awareness about the unfair police practice of carding by writing about his own 50 carding experiences. Carding happens when police racially profile people on the street, stopping them without any reason to review their identification and add it to a database of persons of interest.

The Death of George Floyd

In 2020, Black Lives Matter protests swept across the globe again. That summer in Minneapolis, a restrained unarmed Black man, George Floyd, was killed when a police officer pressed his knee into Floyd's neck for almost 10 minutes in front of a crowd of people. Floyd's death was recorded by teenager Darnella Frazier. She saw that something was terribly wrong, and in sharing the video, raised global awareness.

A Global Movement

People could not deny the injustice of the murder they saw on the news and their devices. Due to the social isolation brought about by the COVID-19 pandemic, many people also had time to really think about what kind of society they wanted to live in. They wondered how it was fair that the power of the police could be used to end the life of a man who could not even fight back.

Anger and pain over Floyd's death added to that already felt about the deaths of other Black people at the hands of the police, police power and anti-Black racism in general. Between 15 and 20 million people protested in the street just in the U.S., and people in Canada and across the globe protested in solidarity.

Receiving Justice

In a historic April 2021 decision, the former officer who caused Floyd's death was convicted of murder. While the trial was taking place, the Black Lives Matter movement was nominated for a Nobel Peace Prize for rallying people around the world to address racism where they live.

Issue: Representation in Society

Many people see themselves and their stories in the television they watch, the books they read and the political and professional leaders around them. However, this is not the case for most Black people in Canada. Canadians are not routinely exposed to positive images of Black people, so Black Canadians rarely see examples of their culture or their contributions. When we do not know their stories, we fill in the missing information with ideas that might not be true.

Representation helps us to know who we are, that we are valued and what we might be able to do in the future.

Why Does Representation Matter?

Everyone deserves to feel seen and understood. Without positive images, Black youth can doubt their own abilities or end up leaving school early because they do not feel engaged in the process. It harms their ability to plan a profession when they do not see other Black people working in the fields they want to work in. People of all backgrounds develop an unbalanced perspective when only the stories of white Canadians are told. Representation helps to show us all what is possible.

Black History on the Screen and Stage

Some Black Canadian artists use movies and theatre to tell their own stories. Filmmakers such as Sylvia Hamilton and Jennifer Hodge de Silva have uncovered almost forgotten stories from Black history. Montreal's Black Theatre Workshop and Toronto's Obsidian Theatre Company perform plays with Black Canadian themes, train young actors and tour schools.

Who's on Top?

Despite facing challenges to success, many Black individuals have managed to achieve high positions. Some of the most successful and recognizable people in North America, especially in sports and entertainment, are Black, but they represent a small percentage. Their success is important, but we cannot assume that all Black people are doing well. Black people are still not represented at all levels in all professions.

The Dangers of Stereotypes

It's important for people of all backgrounds to see Black people succeeding. For non-Black people, a lack of positive images or information may support stereotypes about Black people and cause them to blame Black people or to feel they deserve the poor or inequitable treatment they receive. Without broad representation, we allow the same wrong ideas to persist.

Did You Know

In 2018, activist Viola Desmond was named a National Historic Person by the government and her image appears on the 10-dollar bill.

Danté Bazard · Jason Drew Harrow

Vinessa Antoine · Annamie Paul · Alexandra Bastiany · Kassim Doumbia

If You Can See It, You Can Be It!

What do a mayor from small-town New Brunswick, a Montreal doctor and a chart-topping Scarborough rapper all have in common? They are just a few examples of the many Black Canadians achieving long overdue "firsts" in their fields today. Not only are these trailblazers making important contributions to science, politics, arts and more, they are also breaking down barriers and creating new paths for others to follow.

- The first Black Canadian woman to lead a prime-time television series was Vinessa Antoine in the 2019 CBC series *Diggstown*.

- Danté Bazard became the first Black commissioner of Prince Edward Island's Human Rights Commission in 2020. Commissioners are responsible for promoting and protecting human rights in the province.

- In 2020, Annamie Paul became the first Black Canadian and first Jewish woman to be elected leader of a federal party in Canada.

- Jason Drew Harrow, known onstage as Kardinal Offishall or Kardi, is a rapper and music executive from Scarborough. In 2021, he was appointed Senior Vice President of Artists and Repertoire (A&R) at Universal Music, making him the first Black Canadian senior music executive.

- Montreal doctor Alexandra Bastiany became the first Black woman interventional cardiologist in Canada in 2020. Interventional cardiologists are specially trained to perform complex operations on the heart.

- In 2020, the New Brunswick town of Shippagan elected the first Black mayor in the province's history, Kassim Doumbia.

PROFILE : Masai Ujiri and the Toronto Raptors

In 2013, Nigerian Canadian Masai Ujiri became general manager of the Toronto Raptors. While 75–80% of NBA players are Black, Ujiri is one of only a small handful of Black executives in the NBA.

Everyone was a Raptors fan when they won the 2019 NBA Finals! They represented us all as Canadians and we shared in that pride in winning together. However, when Ujiri tried to join his winning team on the court to congratulate them after the game, he was shoved and kept back by a white security guard. Why? Perhaps he did not fit the guard's biased idea of what an NBA president looks like. Representation can help combat this kind of prejudice.

Honouring Black Heritage All Year

There are many ways to learn about Black Canadian history and culture. Great books and films provide background on the experiences of Black Canadians. You can also join with others and go to a museum or festival, sports game or theatre, to celebrate and share special times both during and beyond Black History Month. We all benefit and feel included when we see ourselves reflected, and we can have fun and learn new information by celebrating Black heritage all year.

Did You Know

In 2021, Toronto Metropolitan University renamed its faculty of law the Lincoln Alexander School of Law to encourage the development of lawyers who value diversity and inclusion.

January 21: Lincoln Alexander Day

The Honourable Lincoln Alexander was the first Black Canadian to be elected as a Member of Parliament (in 1968) and the first person of colour to be appointed as a lieutenant-governor (in 1985). To honour his legacy, the first annual Lincoln Alexander Day was celebrated on January 21, 2015 (his birthday), across Canada. Throughout his career, Alexander championed youth and education, and fought for racial equality. Celebrate by learning more about the man and his legacy.

Did You Know

In 1995, February was declared Black History Month across Canada thanks to the work of Dr. Daniel G. Hill and Rosemary Sadlier of the Ontario Black History Society, and MP Jean Augustine.

February: Black History Month

Black History Month provides an opportunity for everyone to learn more about the contributions and achievements of Black people in Canada. In school, it is a time when the reading and learning that has been done all year can be pulled together and shared with others. In the community, cultural groups, corporations and media offer special events, theatre and dance, as well as films or concerts, to celebrate this important reality: Black people are an essential part of Canada's past, present and future. Celebrate by joining with others in honour of all that you have discovered.

March 21: International Day for the Elimination of Racial Discrimination

On March 21, 1960, 69 South Africans protesting apartheid were brutally killed by police. Now the date is recognized internationally to help build a global culture of equality and anti-discrimination. Celebrate by joining a peaceful protest, finding an organization doing anti-racism work or writing to a politician about issues that are important to you.

July 18: Nelson Mandela International Day

An honorary Canadian citizen, Nelson Mandela inspired people around the world with his fight against racism and apartheid in South Africa. In 2010, the United Nations held the first Mandela Day to celebrate his life and work. Volunteer in your community to honour his legacy.

July & August: Toronto Caribbean Carnival

In the Caribbean, people celebrate Carnival in February, just before the Christian season of Lent. In 1967, Caribbean Canadians and other Black Canadians created a celebration which combined elements of Carnival with the 100th anniversary of Canada and Emancipation Day. Caribana, as it was originally known, has become the largest festival of its kind in North America. Groups prepare all year for the parade, with its steel-drum music, fantastic costumes and non-stop dancing. More than 1 million people attend Caribana from all over North America. Similar celebrations take place in Halifax, Montreal, Windsor and other cities across Canada.

Did You Know

In 1950s Toronto, a group of passionate women created CANEWA, or the Canadian Negro Women's Association. They held the first celebration of Black History Month and an event they called the Calypso Carnival – a model for what would later become Caribana!

Every year in July, people gather for the Africville Reunion in the parkland where the town once stood to remember a special community. Africville was a Black community on the north side of Halifax. Although its story is sad, it should be remembered.

Starting in 1848, Africville attracted Black people from across Nova Scotia who were looking for jobs in Halifax. The town grew to 400 residents by 1951. It was a tight-knit community with the Baptist church at its centre. Some Africville residents worked on trading ships, while others helped to construct Halifax buildings. Some people started their own businesses and owned houses and land.

But problems began almost immediately. In the 1850s, a railway cut through the community. Although the residents paid taxes to Halifax, the city never provided water, sewage or police services. Instead, it located factories, a prison and a garbage dump beside the community. To any outsider, Africville looked like a slum.

In the 1960s, without consulting the residents, Halifax's city council decided to get rid of Africville. Black community leaders protested loudly, saying the residents didn't want to leave. Instead, they needed and deserved the services they'd been denied. However, Africville's houses were destroyed and the people were moved. They were promised better homes, but their new houses were often worse.

The spirit of Africville lives on in the memory of Black Nova Scotians. In 2002, Africville was declared a National Historic Site in recognition of its importance to Black Canadian culture.

August 1: Emancipation Day

In July 1833, following successful slave rebellions in the U.S. and Caribbean and the advocacy of abolitionists, the first act to end slavery in British-controlled countries around the world was passed. In Canada, the law went into effect on August 1, 1834, making it possible for enslaved Africans already in Canada, as well as those who made their way here, to be free. It sparked spontaneous outpourings of joy, gratitude and celebration at the time.

In recent times, August 1st has become a day to celebrate freedom through music, dance, art, community education, worship and activism. Beginning in 1932, in Windsor, Ontario, Walter Perry hosted the largest such celebrations in North America, attracting speakers, performers and thousands of attendees from the U.S. and Canada.

Celebrate by joining or creating an Emancipation Day event in your area and considering what freedom means to you.

Did You Know

August 1st was officially recognized as Emancipation Day nationwide in 2021 thanks to the work of Rosemary Sadlier, Senator Wanda Thomas Bernard and MP Majid Jowhari.

December 26–January 1: Kwanzaa

Kwanzaa is a non-religious celebration created by Dr. Maulana Karenga in the U.S. It started in 1966, following the 1965 race riots in the Watts area of Los Angeles, to address the harm caused to the Black community and bring healing in a non-commercial way. Kwanzaa has grown to a global celebration of the African family, community and culture through an appreciation of African symbols and values. Celebrate Kwanzaa by attending a Kwanzaa event in the community or at home.

Did You Know

Kwanzaa is a Swahili word taken from the phrase matunda ya kwanza, which means "first fruits."

Conclusion

When we learn about how people throughout history have dealt with troubling circumstances, overcome huge challenges and changed society for the better, it connects us to a long story of resilient people who are just like us. When all Canadians learn about Black history, we gain a more balanced understanding of ourselves.

For readers who do not have Black ancestry, Black history can help show how inequities in our current society connect to events from generations ago and provide a more accurate picture of the contributions of many groups to this nation. It was not just men or just Europeans who created the society we know today. It took the efforts of many diverse groups — often championing causes that most touched their experience — including people of African descent.

For Black readers, knowing your history helps to underscore your connection to this country and to world history. It is encouraging to know that others who have gone before made improvements that help everyone.

By knowing our history, and by drawing inspiration from the many incredible figures in Black Canadian history, we can all help to make Canada a more inclusive place to live for Black Canadians and everyone!

Yesterday, Today and Tomorrow

Canada's Black population boasts many skilled and talented people who have achieved fame in a variety of fields. Some have overcome significant challenges in order to make important contributions to Canada, such as Michaëlle Jean, the first Black Canadian to serve as Governor General of Canada.

Many young Black people are following in her footsteps to help shape the nation's future. They still have to fight racism and prejudice, but if they have the strength and courage to keep trying, they will make Canada a better country. Here are just a few of the many well-known Black Canadians.

Randell Adjei, a poet and activist from Scarborough, changed his life after being arrested at age 12. In Grade 8, he connected to the messages found in poetry. At 19, he used his experiences of feeling silenced and marginalized to create an artist incubator for youth called R.I.S.E., Reaching Intelligent Souls Everywhere. He coaches poetry workshops, speaks in schools and gives performances. In 2021, he became the first Poet Laureate of Ontario.

Born in Barbados in 1960, **John Alleyne** studied ballet at the National Ballet School in Toronto. He became a popular solo dancer with Canada's National Ballet after joining the company in 1984. Alleyne then became a talented choreographer who created powerful new ballets. In 1992, this award-winning dancer was appointed artistic director of Ballet British Columbia.

Uzoma Asagwara is from Winnipeg and their parents are Nigerian. While pursuing a Psychiatric Nursing degree, they also excelled in basketball. After graduating, they played on the Canadian National Basketball Team. In 2019, Uzoma channelled their advocacy work in education, poverty and health into politics and became one of the first three Black MLAs (Member of the Legislative Assembly) elected in Manitoba as well as the first Black queer MLA and the first gender non-conforming MLA.

Called "the world's fastest human," **Donovan Bailey** has been clocked running at a speed of 43.6 km/h (27 m.p.h.). Born in 1967 in Jamaica, Bailey grew up in Oakville, Ontario. As a sprinter, Bailey won a gold medal in the 100-metre race at the 1996 Olympics in Atlanta, setting a world record of 9.84 seconds. He was also a member of the Canadian 4 x 100 relay team that won gold at the same Olympic Games.

Born in Jamaica in 1930, **Rosemary Brown** came to Canada as a student. She soon found herself involved in politics, becoming the first Black Canadian woman elected to the British Columbia legislature. Brown served as a member of the New Democratic Party until 1986. She taught at Simon Fraser University in British Columbia and was appointed Chief Commissioner of the Ontario Human Rights Commission. Brown died in 2003.

Carrie Best of New Glasgow, Nova Scotia, was the publisher of a newspaper called the *Clarion* in the 1940s and 1950s. Best was a fearless journalist who demanded fair treatment for Black people. By making sure that Black Canadians were served in restaurants and admitted to theatres, Best helped make Canada a better place to live. She received the Order of Canada in recognition of her fight for her community.

Soprano **Measha Brueggergosman** was only 20-years-old in 1998 when she starred in a new Canadian opera called *Beatrice Chancy*. Born in Fredericton, New Brunswick, Brueggergosman has since had a brilliant international career. She often ends her concerts by singing Black spirituals that celebrate her roots.

Jully Black (Jullyann Inderia Gordon) is a singer, songwriter and actress from Toronto who received her first Juno award shortly before she was signed by a label. Raised by her mother in the Pentecostal tradition and choir, she expanded her musical interests to include soul, R&B, pop and reggae. She has written for or collaborated with Kardinal Offishall, Destiny's Child and Sean Paul. She has starred in theatre productions and is a beloved TV and radio host and panellist.

Born in Nova Scotia in 1960, **George Elliott Clarke** has received many awards for his poetry and is also known as a playwright and screenwriter. In 1997, Clarke wrote the libretto (words) for James Rolfe's opera, *Beatrice Chancy*. The story takes place in Nova Scotia's Annapolis Valley in 1801, when slavery was still a way of life. The opera's first performances starred Measha Brueggergosman.

Trinidad-born **Dionne Brand** came to Toronto, Ontario, in 1970 when she was just 17-years-old. Now she's a well-known writer, filmmaker and human rights activist. Brand's books include *Land to Light On*, which won a Governor General's Award, and *Earth Magic*, a poetry collection for children. In 2009, Brand was named the Poet Laureate of Toronto. She was admitted to the Order of Canada in 2017.

Edmonton-born **Eleanor (Proctor) Collins** is known as Canada's First Lady of Jazz. A talented vocalist steeped in gospel music, she has a sharply trained musical ear and voice. She moved to Vancouver in 1938, married and began performing on CBC radio with her family. By 1955 she had her own television show, making her the first Black musical performer in North America to host her own national television series.

Deborah Cox was born in Toronto in 1974. Inspired by Black singers such as Gladys Knight and Bob Marley, Cox became Canada's first Black female rhythm and blues diva. In 1992, she performed at the inauguration of the new U.S. president, Bill Clinton. In 2022 she was inducted into Canada's Music Hall of Fame – the first Black woman to be inducted.

Scarborough-born **Andre De Grasse** is an outstanding athlete. In 2016, he became the only Canadian sprinter to win three medals in a single Olympics. His mother was a sprinter in Trinidad and Tobago, and his father is from Barbados. De Grasse's coach, former Olympian Tony Sharpe, first noticed his natural talent in high school. De Grasse soon conquered the 100 metre in under 10 seconds (at 9.97), and then the 200 metre in under 20 seconds (19.62). He has six Olympic medals – the most of any Canadian male athlete.

The Caribbean tradition of storytelling followed **Rita Cox** from Trinidad and Tobago to Canada. When Cox tells her ghost stories, fables and animal stories, children gather round. This storyteller also founded the Black Heritage and West Indies Collection, one of the most important collections of writings about and by Black people. Cox received the Governor General's 1992 Commemorative Medal for her contributions to Canada, and in 2022, a Toronto school was renamed in her honour.

Aubrey Drake Graham, or **Drake**, is known as the actor, rapper and musician who helped to place Toronto on the world stage. After starring in the CTV television series *Degrassi: The Next Generation* as a teen, he left to pursue music. He has since sold more than 170 million records and is the highest ranked musician for digital singles in R&B, rap and hip hop. Drake also founded the OVO Sound record label and is a global ambassador for the Toronto Raptors. In 2021, he was named Artist of the Decade by *Billboard*.

In 1990, **Charmaine Crooks** of North Vancouver became the first Canadian woman to run 800 metres in less than two minutes. Born in Jamaica, the sprinter made the Canadian Olympic team in 1980, when she was only 16. Crooks has since competed in a record five Olympic Games. Today, she's a television host and public speaker.

It's your world, so take part in it, and never give up on your dream.

Dr. Juliet Daniel is a biology professor and cancer researcher at McMaster University. She discovered a gene she named Kaiso, which is responsible for how genes grow and connect to each other. Kaiso is an African/Caribbean word that means "let's join." Her work helps us understand how genetics impact the risk of getting cancer, especially for women of African ancestry. Her work is so important that it has been referred to by other medical researchers more than 4000 times!

Calgary-born **Esi Edugyan**, the daughter of Ghanaian parents, is an award-winning novelist and writer. While her first novel, *The Second Life of Samuel Tyne*, was very successful, she couldn't find a publisher for her second book. She gave up on that manuscript and wrote *Half-Blood Blues*, which won the 2011 Scotiabank Giller Prize and was shortlisted for the Man Booker Prize. Edugyan won the Giller Prize a second time for her 2018 novel *Washington Black*.

Ferguson Jenkins is a famous baseball player born in Chatham, Ontario, in 1943. A major-league pitcher, he struck out more than 3000 batters during his career with the Texas Rangers, the Chicago Cubs and the Boston Red Sox. In 1991, Jenkins was the first Black Canadian inducted into the Baseball Hall of Fame.

During the final men's hockey game of the 2002 Olympic Games, **Jarome Iginla** scored two goals against the U.S. team to ensure Canada's gold-medal victory. This powerful forward was born in 1977 in Edmonton, Alberta, and is a six-time NHL all-star. He retired in 2019 and was inducted into the Hockey Hall of Fame in 2020.

Vladimir Guerrero Ramos Jr. was born in Montreal, where his Hall-of-Famer father played for the Montreal Expos, but soon moved to the Dominican Republic with his mother. He spent his summers with his dad and showed the same talent for baseball. In 2015, the 17-year-old was signed by the Blue Jays. He was identified as Minor League Player of the Year in 2018 and was voted MVP of the 2021 All-Star game – the youngest in history.

Namugenyi "Nam" Kiwanuka arrived in Canada in 1983 from a refugee camp following the Ugandan Civil War. Entering the media, she has reported for CNN, BET, NBA TV and MuchMusic. She now co-hosts *The Agenda* with Steve Paikin and hosts *The Thread with Nam Kiwanuka*, both on TVO. She has volunteered with War Child Canada and Journalists for Human Rights.

Stephan James is a Toronto-born actor from a Jamaican family. He started in the Canadian television series *Degrassi: The Next Generation*, leading to various roles and a Canadian Screen Award for Best Actor for portraying American Olympian Jesse Owens in *Race*. When he portrayed John Lewis in the Oscar-nominated *Selma*, his position as a rising star was secured. To extend opportunities, mentorship and funding for Black talent across Canada, he created The Black Academy with his brother, Shamier Anderson.

African immigrant **Daniel Igali** won Canada's first gold medal in wrestling at the Olympic Games in 2000. Igali was born in Nigeria in 1974, but in 1994, he left his 20 brothers and sisters behind to compete in the Commonwealth Games in Victoria, B.C. He stayed in Canada to train. When Igali won his Olympic gold medal, he joyfully kissed Canada's flag.

Nova Scotia has produced many excellent Black boxers. **Sam Langford**, born in 1884 at Weymouth Falls, was a truly great heavyweight boxer. He held the heavyweight championships of England, Spain and Mexico – even though he was only 167 cm (5 ft. 6 in.) tall and weighed just 71 kg (157 lb.)!

Daurene Lewis is a seventh-generation Nova Scotian from Annapolis Royal. (One of her ancestors, Rose Fortune, became Canada's first policewoman around 1783.) Lewis graduated from Dalhousie University in Halifax, and later taught nursing. From 1984 to 1988, she was the mayor of Annapolis Royal, the first Black woman mayor in North America.

After arriving in Toronto from Nova Scotia, **Beverly Mascoll** soon realized the growing demand for Black hair care products and relaxers. In 1970, she started Mascoll Beauty Supply Ltd. and began selling products from her car. She opened her first store in 1973, becoming Johnson Products' sole Canadian distributor. By 1985, Mascoll Beauty Supply was a multi-million-dollar company supplying national chains. In 1996, she created the Beverly Mascoll Community Foundation to aid women and youth.

An Afro-Latina Muslim born in Panama, **Ginella Massa** is a reporter and anchor. She became Canada's first hijab-wearing reporter while at CTV News in Kitchener, Ontario, in 2015, and the first hijabi anchor in 2016 at CityNews Toronto. In 2020, she joined CBC as a special correspondent for *The National* and host of the show *Canada Tonight*, which launched in 2021.

Children's author **Tololwa M. Mollel** was born in Tanzania in 1952. Since moving to Edmonton, Alberta, Mollel has published more than 20 books – including *The Orphan Boy* and *Kitoto the Mighty* – and has won many awards. He runs storytelling and drama workshops for children around North America.

Dr. Onye Nnorom was born in Montreal to parents from Trinidad and Tobago and Nigeria. Nnorom worked hard to graduate from Concordia University and then attended medical school at McGill and completed a Masters of Public Health at the University of Toronto. Her work as a family doctor, public health specialist and teacher focuses on the social determinants of health, in particular how racism affects the health of Black Canadians and other racialized Canadians.

Siphesihle "Siphe" November is a South African–born dancer and choreographer who was invited to join The National Ballet of Canada in 2017 at 18-years-old. He became a principal dancer by 2021 at 22-years-of-age. In 2019, he received the International Erik Bruhn Prize and he choreographed his first piece in 2020. His repertoire includes *The Nutcracker*, *Giselle*, *Chroma*, *The Sleeping Beauty* and *The Dream*.

Vancouver's **Anthonia Ogundele** supports both the past and the future. Using her background in urban planning, she founded the Hogan's Alley Land Trust in 2016 to retain the Black history of the area. She is the founder of a STEM learning centre for youth called Ethos Lab. It introduces new technologies and innovations to youth ages 12 to 18 and is home to Canada's first Black-led virtual reality environment.

World-famous jazz pianist **Oscar Peterson** was born in Montreal in 1925. At 14, he won a national contest for amateur musicians. Peterson was still in his twenties when he dazzled the audience with his flying fingers at New York's famous Carnegie Hall. A composer as well as a jazz pianist, Peterson won many awards and was a Companion of the Order of Canada. He died in 2007.

Playwright **Djanet Sears** wrote Canada's first stage play by a person of African descent, called *Afrika Solo*. Born in England, Sears moved with her family to Saskatoon, Saskatchewan, when she was 15. She won a Governor General's Award for *Harlem Duet* in 1998. Sears was a founding member of Obsidian Theatre, which specializes in African and Caribbean Canadian drama.

Clement Virgo, originally from Jamaica, moved to Canada when he was 11. He studied filmmaking at the Norman Jewison Canadian Film Centre, north of Toronto. The first film Virgo directed, *Rude*, won the Best Feature Film prize at the Toronto Film Festival. He has released four feature films and directed for television.

The Weeknd (Abel Makkonen Tesfaye), a Toronto-born child of Ethiopian immigrants, began his career in 2009 uploading original music to YouTube. Signed to a label within two years, he went on to become one of the world's bestselling artists. Wanting to support his culture, The Weeknd helped fund the University of Toronto's Ethiopic studies program, and in 2020 he launched Black HXOUSE, which provides skills and networking programs for people of colour.

The first really successful Canadian rap artist was **Maestro Fresh Wes**. He was born in Toronto in 1968 to Guyanese parents. His first album sold more than 150 000 copies in Canada, and on his second album, he rapped about the Black Canadian identity. The Maestro won the first Canadian Juno Award for Best Rap Recording in 1991.

Toronto-born **Julien Christian Lutz**, or **Director X**, worked on several film productions before moving into music videos in the 1990s. He has directed dozens of music videos, creating visually distinctive material for Jay-Z, Nelly Furtado, Justin Bieber, Drake, Nicki Minaj and Rihanna. In 2015, his Nova Scotia–shot feature film debut, *Across the Line*, starring Stephan James, won the Best Atlantic Feature film. He launched the production company Fela in 2020.

OTHER BLACK CANADIAN FIRSTS

- In 1990, **Zanana Akande** became the first Black woman elected to the Legislative Assembly of Ontario and the first woman from the African Diaspora to serve as a provincial Cabinet minister in Canada.
- **Jean Augustine**, of Ontario, was the first Black Canadian woman in Canada's Parliament (in 1993) and in the Cabinet (in 2002).
- **Anne Cools**, of Ontario, became Canada's first Black senator in 1984.
- **George Dixon**, who was born in Nova Scotia, was the first Black person to win a World Boxing Championship, in 1890.
- **Willie O'Ree**, of New Brunswick, became the first Black NHL hockey player in 1958.
- **Corrine Sparks**, from Nova Scotia, was the first Black woman to become a judge in Canada, in 1987.

GLOSSARY

activist: someone who takes action to make social or political change

African Diaspora: the communities of African people and descendants of Africans who are living outside that continent

ally: someone who supports you in what you wish to do

apartheid: a legal system in South Africa between 1948 and 1994 that kept races separate or "apart." All South Africans had to carry passbooks that showed their race and where they could live. Black people could not live in nor travel in white areas without permission in the form of a passbook issued by the government. It was an extreme form of segregation.

Atlantic slave trade: a triangular trade route that enriched European nations. The outward passage, from Europe to Africa, brought manufactured goods in exchange for African people and products. The middle passage took people from Africa across the Atlantic and traded these people for goods manufactured in the Caribbean or the Americas. The return passage brought manufactured goods or other resources back to Europe. Millions of Africans were removed from their birthplace and forced into slavery to build up the economies of Europe.

barrier: something that prevents your progress or restricts your opportunities because of your race, religion, ethnicity or other categories

bias: a belief (usually negative) about an individual or group that is based on subjective feeling rather than knowledge

Black: describes people of African descent who typically have dark skin, though Black people have a wide range of skin tones

Creole: during slavery and colonization, the children of mixed European and African descent were called Creole. The languages that were created through this early contact were also called Creole. Now Creole can mean the people, culture, languages and foods that all began with this early mixing.

emancipation: the act of freeing someone from slavery

enslaved person: a human being who is considered to be the property of another person. An enslaved person is forced to work for free and has no rights to their life or their labour. No one is born a slave – a slave is created by ideas, laws, power and social practice.

equality: the idea that everyone has the same opportunities

equity: the idea that not everyone has the same opportunities, so barriers must be removed for certain groups to achieve equality with others

marginalization: isolation or exclusion of some people from society

power: being able to make decisions and get what you want. When power is used unfairly, people can be directly harmed or not have their needs considered or met.

prejudice: long-held negative ideas about others because they are different than you in terms of race, religion, sex, class, ability, age or other categories

privilege: an advantage that only some people have based on their race, gender, class, wealth or position in society. If a privilege goes unchallenged, it can become a part of our society for some people and over time seem "normal."

racism and anti-Black racism: systems and actions based on prejudiced ideas of the superiority of one race over others. Anti-Black racism directs negative ideas and actions toward people of African origin.

segregation: separating groups of people based on race, ethnicity or class through laws and ideas, and treating certain groups worse than others

social determinants of health: non-medical factors that impact your physical and mental health. We know that smoking can be bad for our health and should be avoided. Social determinants of health are unavoidable things, such as where you were born, how free of harmful substances your neighbourhood might be, how healthy your water or food supply is or what pollutants you are exposed to at school or work.

stereotype: a belief that all people from a group are the same based on very little knowledge or experience

INDEX